BARRY BUCKNELL ABOUT THE HOUSE

BARRY BUCKNELL

Illustrated by
Brian Craker

INDEPENDENT TELEVISION BOOKS LTD, LONDON

INDEPENDENT TELEVISION BOOKS LTD, LONDON
247 Tottenham Court road,
London W1P 0AU

© Barry Bucknell 1976

ISBN 0 900 72752 7

St. Stephen's (Bristol) Press Ltd
Poplar Road, Warmley, Bristol.

CONTENTS

Introduction

The aim of this book is to tackle all the Do it Yourself jobs which crop up most frequently around the house, the garden, and the garage, and which almost everyone these days, enthusiastic handyman or not, has to tackle.

I have tried to give the simplest methods of dealing with these jobs, sometimes unorthordox methods, and always a short cut wherever this can be effective and save valuable time.

I have concentrated on the least expensive and the most basic tools which require the minimum skill. Even when the Do it Yourself enthusiasm leads you on to greater heights, and the purchase of more advanced tools, it may still be worthwhile keeping this basic kit separate and readily available.

If you are just starting in this field the likelihood is that provided the jobs you have to tackle through necessity go smoothly and successfully and give you a sense of achievement your range and enjoyment will steadily increase.

I hope this book will give help and encouragement in this direction.

Barry Bucknell

TOOLS
Household tool kit

This is a suggestion for a basic tool kit which will deal with the bulk of the small jobs around the house. Even if you have a much more extensive kit in the workshop it may well be an advantage to keep this kit somewhere handy.

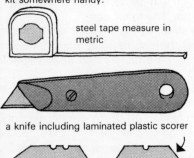

steel tape measure in metric

a knife including laminated plastic scorer

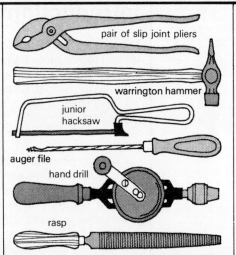

pair of slip joint pliers

warrington hammer

junior hacksaw

auger file

hand drill

rasp

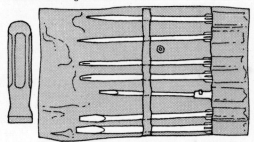

screwdriver kit with interchangeable blades including bradawl

With this list it will be handy to have: **roll electrical sticky tape for insulating** and other purpose, selection of wall plugs and tap washers, selection of adhesives, fuse wire, fuses, candle (for making drawers, etc slide easily).

Hints on use of some basic tools

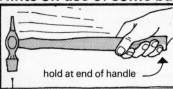

hold at end of handle

Hammers
Clean face of hammer by rubbing on floor or sandpaper. Hold hammer at end of handle, using wrist, arm and shoulder.
Use block to protect surfaces and improve leverage of claw hammer when extracting nails. Same with pincers. Cross pein hammer helps to start nails. Pin hammer is lighter version. (Pin push also makes it easier to start pins). Can be held in a comb.

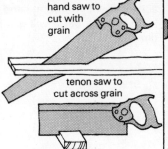

hand saw to cut with grain

tenon saw to cut across grain

Tenon saw and hand saw
Keep eye and arm in line to keep cut at right angles. Low angle for ordinary cut. Hold higher for cutting with grain (ripping). Keep guard on saw when not in use. Can have it sharpened professionally.

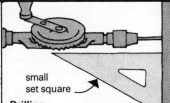

small set square

Drilling
Can use set square to make sure you are drilling at right angles or get someone to check by eye. Twist drills not really designed for wood, but small sizes can be used. Using carpenter's bit, clamp the work to a waste piece of wood, or drill back from other side when point of bit appears. Power wood bits available for electric drill. Use a countersink bit for sinking screw heads flush.

Power tools

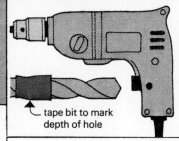

tape bit to mark depth of hole

Power tools can speed up quite ordinary jobs like drilling hard masonry. Check plugs are wired correctly, with earth wire connected if not double insulated, and do not wear loose clothing such as a tie. Never leave power tools plugged in when not in use.

Wall fixings

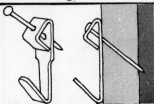

Picture hooks These have hardened steel pins which will penetrate the plaster and softer brickwork and get a good grip—usually adequate for the average picture and they do not damage the wall seriously.

Stick-on hooks Holding power depends on the surface they are stuck to. A paint layer can pull away or plaster disintegrate.

Suction discs These will only support light loads and must be used on a hard smooth surface. If the back is sanded with fine glass paper and a contact adhesive used it will carry more weight.

Wall plugs
Making the hole

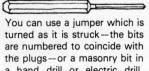

You can use a jumper which is turned as it is struck—the bits are numbered to coincide with the plugs—or a masonry bit in a hand drill or electric drill. Press fairly hard and remove to clear occasionally. Mark the depth you want by sticking on a piece of tape.

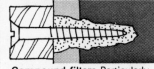

Compound fillers Particularly suitable if hole is too large or distorted. Moisten and knead to a dough and press into the hole with a spike. Make a thread hole before completely set, but do not drive the screw finally in until completely hard.

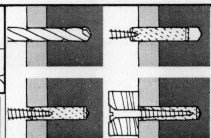

Jute plugs The traditional plug still widely used is numbered to fit the screw number and should be a suitable depth to take the screw when the plug is sunk below the plaster. Having made the hole, insert the screw one or two threads so that you can pack the plug below the plaster. Screw in further to expand the plug then remove the screw and screw on the fitting.

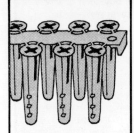

Plastic plugs There are many varieties. The one illustrated has the advantage that the plug will take a range of screws. Fitting is similar to previous plug. Will give some grip in a hollow wall.

Hollow wall fixings Here there is an even wider variety.

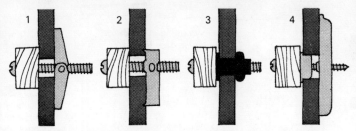

1   2   3   4

1 Spring toggle Needs larger hole to push through—does not remain in place with screw removed, but easy to use. Spans largest area.

2 Gravity toggle Smaller hole, does not remain.

3 Rubber sleeved anchor Very good grip. Slight ridge on surface.

Remains when unscrewed. Particularly good for walls which are solid but of soft material.

4 Nylon toggle Fairly small hole. Needs nylon retaining strap cutting off. Expanding or spreading plastics. Takes ordinary wood screws.

Very heavy fixings More expensive anchor bolts take high loads—clothes lines etc.

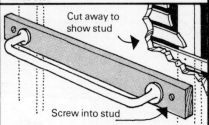

Cut away to show stud

Screw into stud

Fixing to a lath and plaster wall Often the safest fixing is a batten screwed to the upright frames (studs) spanning two or more with the fitting screwed to the batten. Find the position of upright by tapping to find where the wall sounds solid and then probing with a bradawl.

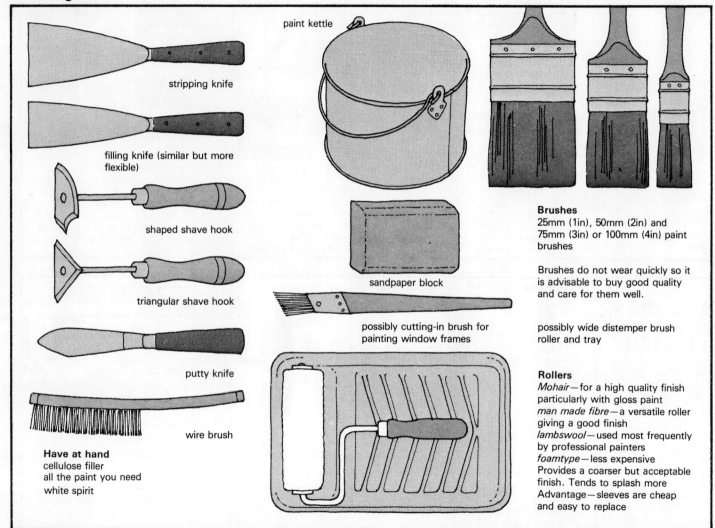

stripping knife

filling knife (similar but more flexible)

shaped shave hook

triangular shave hook

putty knife

wire brush

Have at hand
cellulose filler
all the paint you need
white spirit

paint kettle

sandpaper block

possibly cutting-in brush for painting window frames

Brushes
25mm (1in), 50mm (2in) and 75mm (3in) or 100mm (4in) paint brushes

Brushes do not wear quickly so it is advisable to buy good quality and care for them well.

possibly wide distemper brush roller and tray

Rollers
Mohair—for a high quality finish particularly with gloss paint
man made fibre—a versatile roller giving a good finish
lambswool—used most frequently by professional painters
foamtype—less expensive
Provides a coarser but acceptable finish. Tends to splash more
Advantage—sleeves are cheap and easy to replace

Types of paint

Covering capacity:
(A) 13-15 square metres per litre (5 litres / 80-90 sq. yards)
(B) 14-16 square metres per litre (5 litres / 85-95 sq. yards)

High gloss
Interior and exteriors. Specially weather resistant. On a good base with little colour change, thixotropic (jelly) gloss can cover with one coat—non drip, no undercoat.

Eggshell finish
interiors. Mainly for woodwork. For walls vinyl is easier to use.

Vinyl water-based paint
Interiors and exteriors. Water thinned, so equipment can be cleaned with water. Can now obtain gloss, but not as high as an alkyd gloss. No undercoat, but may need primer on absorbent surface. Needs attention to temperature—follow instructions.

Emulsion paint
Interiors and exteriors. Particularly suitable for walls and ceilings; easy to use; inexpensive. Use oil based primer on powdery surfaces.

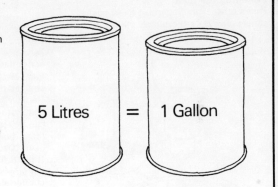

5 Litres = 1 Gallon

Brush care

Brush out and scrape off as much paint as possible. A supply of old newspapers is handy.

With water-based paints clean with warm water with some detergent, rinsing out thoroughly.

With oil-based paints wash in white spirit or in paraffin which is less expensive. A brush cleaner is quicker but more expensive.

Finally wash thoroughly in warm water and detergent. Rinse and dry thoroughly and store in polythene.
For two-pack paints a special solvent is needed.

If you want to store a brush temporarily you can buy plastic containers. The lids can be made to fit most handles by softening them with hot water. These keep the brushes suspended with the bristles just immersed in solvent. Or you can make a container by punching a hole with a screwdriver in a metal screw top, taping the brush in position.

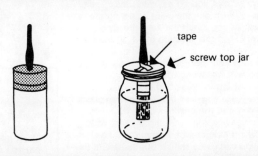

tape

screw top jar

PAINTING
Preparation

Preparing the paint

Paints other than thixotropic (jelly) paints should always be thoroughly stirred. A

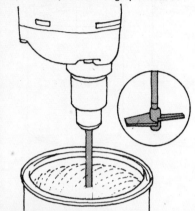

paint stirring attachment for an electric drill is inexpensive and speeds up the stirring. Switch on after immersion and off before taking out and keep at lowest speed. By hand use something flat such as old kitchen knife, flat batten etc, not screwdriver.

Paint which has any particles in it should be strained through muslin or a nylon stocking. Remove the skin from the used can by a neat cut round the outside. Skin forming can be lessened by storing with a close fitting polythene or foil disc floating on the paint. Date stored tins.

If the paint tin has no handle, either stand the tin inside a paint-kettle or make a comfortable handle with two straps—one round the tin and the other passing under and over to form a handle. Tape the straps together where they cross. If necessary you can tie this on to your ladder.

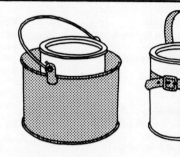

Preparing the room

Remove as much furniture from the room as possible. If you can, lift the carpet and cover the floor with old sheets or thick layers of newspaper. Furniture that you can't shift should be covered with sheets or newspapers.

Painting walls

Brush painting

Dip brush in about 1/3 length of bristles. Tap the tip against the inside of the can. Hold brush near base and using the finger tips apply a light pressure—enough to make the bristles flex.

Brush on in two directions brushing out the paint so that you do not get 'runs'. Then 'line off'—stroke the paint off lifting the brush as you reach the area already painted—in the direction in which the main area lies.

Arrange your painting so that a paint edge is always wet when you return to it.

For 'cutting in'—painting close to an edge—use a special brush or put an elastic band round the bristles of a small brush. Alternatively you can mask an area with masking tape or with shiny insulating tape, or you can use a shield. But be careful to see that paint does not get underneath.

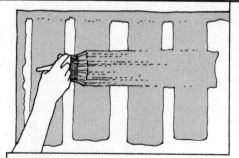

Roller painting

Use roller tray and roll surplus paint off roller on tray. Roll in three directions. Paint in small squares trying to keep the edges wet.

Clean rollers and trays in the same way as brushes (see page 9).

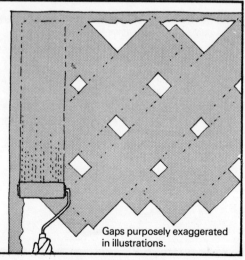

Gaps purposely exaggerated in illustrations.

Painting woodwork

Strip the paint only where absolutely necessary due to bad adhesion or severe bubbling.
Sponge down with warm water and detergent and rinse with clean water.
For new wood or if you have had to strip, rub down, dust, give two coats, patent knotting over knots and resinous areas. Make sure wood is dry. Then prime and apply further coats as recommended by manufacturer.
Paint the skirting after the walls, then windows, doors, etc.
Remove residues of polish with white spirit and clean cloths. Wash and rub down as usual. All traces of silicone polish must be removed by rubbing down with wet and dry glasspaper and cleaning with white spirit.
If wood has been stained try painting a small area and allow to dry.

Painting a door

Follow the order shown working towards the middle when painting panels. See that paint does not build up on the edges.

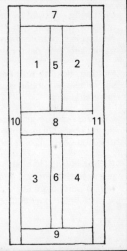

Painting a sash window

With the bottom of the frame raised you can lower the top and paint the bottom third. Then drop the bottom and paint the top, finishing with the bottom. Allowing paint to build up around the edges of windows can prevent them shutting properly. Before adding more paint, test with thin cardboard to see what clearance you have. If not enough, either don't paint edge or first strip old paint. Prime and repaint.

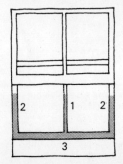
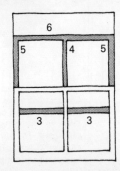
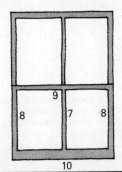

Painting other surfaces

It is possible to paint over well adhering *wallpaper* but it may become detached and metallic colours may bleed through. Check trial area with emulsion paint—if necessary seal as recommended with oil based sealer or strip. Emulsion painting over *wallpaper* can produce bubbles which may disappear on drying. Otherwise you may have to prick them or strip the paper and start again.
Water-soluble distemper should be completely removed by soaking, scraping and sanding.
Plaster which is very porous will need a sealer for oil-based paint. Fill any cracks with cellulose filler or resin wood fill for larger cracks and harder wear. Rub down with abrasive paper (400 wet and dry used wet). A soda block is a coarse abrasive to be used only where drastic cutting down is necessary.

PAINTING
Painting faults

Blistering—caused by moisture trapped underneath or painting in damp atmosphere, or resins from knots, particularly with deep colours in strong sun.

Flaking, scaling and peeling—can sometimes be rubbed down and filled. May need stripping.

Crazing—due to incompatible paints or hard drying coats being applied soon after previous coat.

Bittiness—due to dust or foreign bodies in paint. Rub down wall and repaint. A 'tack rag' (a proprietary sticky pad) wiped over surface before painting helps remove dust.

Bleeding or discolouration—from paint beneath. Strip and seal with aluminium sealer before repainting.

Runs—due to faulty technique; applying too thickly and not brushing out.

Wrinkles—can be rubbed down and repainted. Due to paint being applied too thickly. May have to be stripped.

Colour beneath 'grins' through—due to paint which is too thin or too few coats. Stick to recommended undercoat and do not overthin.

Chalking—not necessarily serious apart from appearance. Outdoor paints are designed to chalk so that rain washes away dirt.

Efflorescence—a white deposit which appears on masonry. May have to strip and use an alkali resistant primer.

Mould appears—clean off and use a fungicidal wash. May have to use a fungicidal paint.

Stripping paint

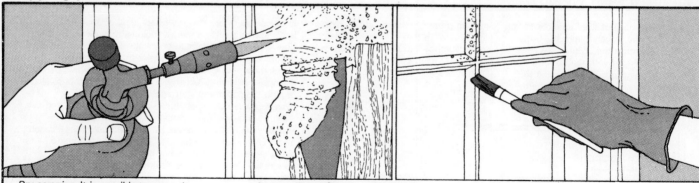

Dry scraping It is possible to use a dry scraper effectively but it needs practice—easy to leave score marks.

Burning off is cheapest and quickest and a bottled gas blowlamp is very convenient. It must not be used on asbestos sheeting,

plaster walls or near glass. Just melt paint without scorching wood and scrape upwards having pail of water beneath to catch droppings. Any charring will have to be rubbed down before painting. Do not rely on newspaper on the floor.

Chemical stripper is more expensive but easy to use and can go close to glass. *Wear rubber gloves and keep eyes protected. Do not leave stopper off near children.* Clean off with white spirit, but follow maker's instructions.

Cracks in plaster

Scrape crack to remove loose pieces and provide good keying for filler.

Brush off dust.

Damp slightly.

Mix filler to cake mix consistency and apply to crack, keeping filling knife – which has a flexible blade – at a shallow angle to the wall.

If the crack is large, more than one application of filler will be needed. Leave rough to provide key for next layer.

Finally sand surface.

Holes in plaster

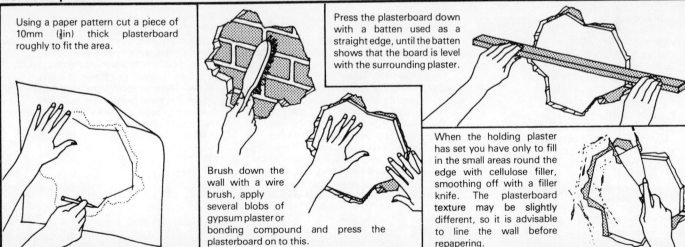

Using a paper pattern cut a piece of 10mm (⅜in) thick plasterboard roughly to fit the area.

Brush down the wall with a wire brush, apply several blobs of gypsum plaster or bonding compound and press the plasterboard on to this.

Press the plasterboard down with a batten used as a straight edge, until the batten shows that the board is level with the surrounding plaster.

When the holding plaster has set you have only to fill in the small areas round the edge with cellulose filler, smoothing off with a filler knife. The plasterboard texture may be slightly different, so it is advisable to line the wall before repapering.

WALLPAPERING
Tools for paperhanging

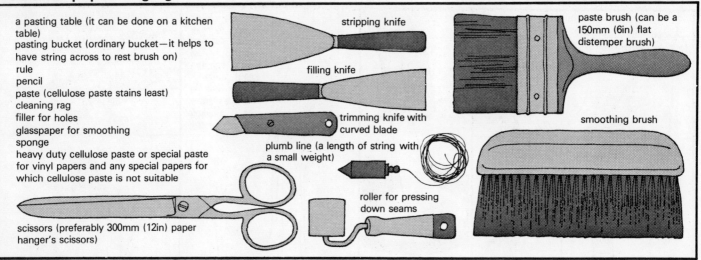

a pasting table (it can be done on a kitchen table)

pasting bucket (ordinary bucket—it helps to have string across to rest brush on)

rule

pencil

paste (cellulose paste stains least)

cleaning rag

filler for holes

glasspaper for smoothing

sponge

heavy duty cellulose paste or special paste for vinyl papers and any special papers for which cellulose paste is not suitable

scissors (preferably 300mm (12in) paper hanger's scissors)

stripping knife

filling knife

trimming knife with curved blade

plumb line (a length of string with a small weight)

roller for pressing down seams

paste brush (can be a 150mm (6in) flat distemper brush)

smoothing brush

Before you start

Ordering paper
A roll is approximately 10.05 metres (11yds) long and 530mm (21ins) wide. Measure the number of widths round room and multiply by height, divide by 10 metres (11yds). Ignore doors and windows unless very large.

Cutting to length
Measure height you want and allow extra 75mm (3ins). Cut off or tear along edge of ruler. Many repeating patterns have a 'drop'. You need to hold roll against first length matching pattern and cutting off waste each time unless you cut from matched alternate rolls.

Preparing the walls
Old paper can be tested for adhesion but it is usually advisable to remove (except from plaster board, which can be difficult). Soak well with a detergent in warm water or a special additive. Scrape off with broad filling knife. If difficult scratch with hacksaw blade or wire brush before soaking. Wash off old paste and lightly sand. Fill cracks (see page 13) and sand. Give absorbent walls coat of glue size (instructions on packet) or of cellulose paste.

A rough wall may need lining horizontally bottom upwards with butt joints, turning about 25mm (1in) round corners. If overpapering, do not join over original joins.

Pasting
Mix paste thoroughly and leave 15 minutes or so. Start with top of paper.

Paste herring bone fashion towards far edge of table with paper overhanging about 6mm (¼in). Leave about 50mm (2in) bare at end. Move paper to table edge nearest you and repeat. Paste edges well. Fold pasted part together. Draw along table and paste remainder. Fold again and allow to soak about 5 minutes for average weight paper.

Hanging wallpaper

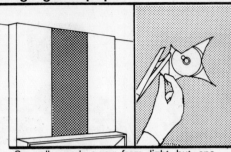 

Generally work away from light but one length must be hung first down centre of chimney breast. Arrange joining up point where mismatch is least obtrusive.

Make pencil marks with plumb line, preferably with assistance to start first length vertically.

Brush on a section at the top and slide against marks, brushing on lightly. Pull away and start again where necessary—there's no hurry. Always wipe off paste as it can damage paintwork.

Cutting round door frames, fire surrounds etc.
Make diagonal cut towards point. Press paper into angle with scissors and cut along crease.

Cutting round switches
Make star cuts from centre—4 for square box, more for round switch. Press in all round and cut as before.

Hanging light
Make hole in paper and hang wire through—star cuts for cutting round.

Inside window recess
Paper recess, first overlapping wall by 25mm (1in). Now hang wallpaper as usual, trimming flush to wall corner of recess.

Blisters and patching
Make star cut with razor blade. Paste flaps and restick. If necessary to patch, tear roughly round edge of patch.

Marking screw holes
Where fitting is removed stick broken matches into holes and press paper over.

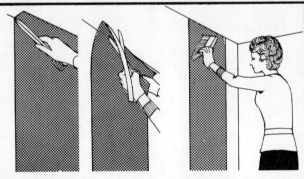

The edges
Brush into the angle at picture rail or cornice. Gently crease in angle with edge of scissors. Pull away and cut along crease. Wipe any excess paste off as you go. Do the same at skirting angles. Hang next length butted up against first. Paper will stretch a little over irregularities.

Angles
When approaching the corner of the room measure between last length hung and angle, at two or three points. Add 6mm ($\frac{1}{4}$in) to greatest measurement. Reduce the width of the next length to this measurement. Mark the width on pasted (and folded) paper at several points and cut along line. Extra 6mm ($\frac{1}{4}$in) will turn corner and next length hung vertically (using a plumbline) will overlap. Slight break in pattern will not be noticed.

On external corners of chimney breasts etc., turn 25mm (1in) round sides and overlap slightly with next length hung vertically.

Ceiling papering
More difficult than wall papering. Scaffold—plank across steps or trestles desirable.

Hang away from light but avoid first length along irregular wall. Have someone hold the other end of a chalked string. Pluck it in the middle and this will mark a straight line. Lengths usually longer so paste in sections and fold concertina-wise holding folds up with cut off broom stick or spare roll of paper moving along as you brush paper on. If you lose direction this is not irrevocable. Pull down section and start again.

FLOOR COVERINGS
Laying lino

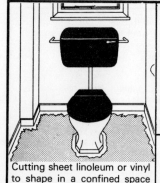

Cutting sheet linoleum or vinyl to shape in a confined space can be difficult. This method makes it easier: Cut or tear brown paper or grey paper felt so that it roughly fits the floor area (the grey paper felt can be used as an underlay).

Slide a wooden block say 50mm x 50mm (2in x 2in) round the walls and all obstructions and holding a pencil against the block mark a line on the pattern. This will be the same shape as the area to be covered but will be 50mm (2in.) smaller than the area to be covered. Take the pattern into another room and attach it to the new floor covering with adhesive tape so that you can reverse the process. Then running the

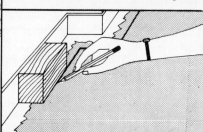

block round the line on the pattern you can draw the actual shape.

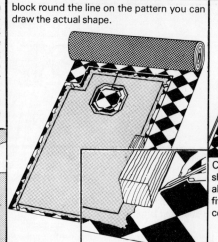

Cut out the covering making a slit behind the pedestal hole to allow the floor covering to be fitted round the pedestal. Floor covering should now fit snugly.

Making a rug non-slip

There are several ways in which you can make rugs non-slip. You can use double sided tape or a special rubber or plastic coated netting underneath. Alternatively there are special gripping strips which can be stuck to the floor underneath the rug.

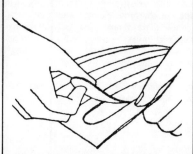

You can also use touch tape patches stuck or pinned to the floor with corresponding patches stuck or sewn to the rug. Always make sure that the floor is clear and free from dust.

Finally you can pin metal strips with turned up teeth onto the floor and hook the rug onto these. This well also help with the problem of curled up edges which can be dangerous.

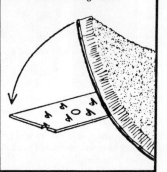

Ring circuit and rewiring a fuse

Although rewiring is the province of the skilled D-I-Y man, it may help you to know how a modern wiring system differs from the old fashioned system. In the latter most outlet sockets were individually wired back to a 15 amp maximum fuse in the main fusebox. Now a number of outlet sockets serving probably 185 sq. metres (1000 sq. ft) of floor area are wired in the form of a ring and connected to a 30 amp fuse in the main fusebox. (A consumer unit can have curcuit breakers which perform the same function as fuses.) These socket outlets take square pin plugs each of which has its own separate fuse which should be the appropriate size for the appliance.

Standard lamps and small appliances 3 amps
Electric irons and medium appliances 3 amps
Electric fires and large appliances 13 amps

An electric cooker has its own wiring and a much larger fuse in the fusebox.

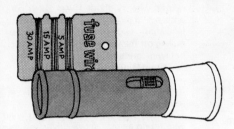

Rewiring a fuse
A fuse is a weak link which is introduced into a circuit to guard against its being overloaded, overheating and possibly causing a fire.
A fuse should therefore never be replaced with one of a higher rating or with any piece of wire.
Fuse wire kept near the fuse box and also a torch or a candle can be a help.

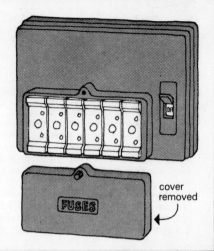

cover removed

four types of rewirable fuse

First remove any equipment you suspect of being faulty or of causing the overload and 'blowing' the fuse.
Switch off at the main switch. Remove the fuse holder from the fusebox (you should have a chart of the fuses on the fuse box cover). Otherwise try each fuse in turn testing the wire for a break with a screwdriver if it is hidden.
Unscrew the terminal screws, replace the wire with one of the same rating, 5 amps for lighting, 10 or 15 amps for power, 30 amps for ring main.

Do not stretch the new wire tightly, wind clockwise round the terminal screws.
If the fuse continues to 'blow' the cause must be investigated. Some less popular fuse holders take cartridge fuses, with fuse wire sealed in.
A circuit breaker performs the same function as a fuse but after it has flipped out, if the fault is cleared it can be switched on again.
Ordinary fuse holders can in some cases be replaced by miniature circuit breakers.
For fuses in plugs see page 18.

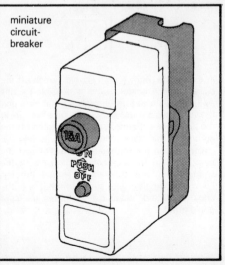

miniature circuit-breaker

ELECTRICITY
Rewiring a plug

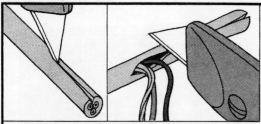

Strip the outer insulation back about 50mm (2in) if you have screw terminals, 40mm (1½in) if you have push in terminals.

As you cut round the outer insulation make sure you do not cut the insulation on the wires.

Cut the end of the outer insulation for about 12.5mm (½in). Pull the wires up to extend the split and cut off the insulation. In some plugs it helps to shorten the live wire and the neutral wire by about 10mm (⅜in). Strip the ends of the wires by cutting round the insulation without cutting the wire and pulling off the insulation by hand, by scissors or plyers (preferably not teeth).

25mm (1in) for screw terminals
10mm (⅜in) for push in terminals

Inexpensive wire strippers do this in one operation.

For screw type terminals (as right) wind the wire round a small screw driver and twist so that you have a fixed loop to put the screw through.

For push in terminals fold the wire over once, push in and tighten.

Finally clamp the flex firmly under the cord grip.

Insert the correct fuse if one is needed.

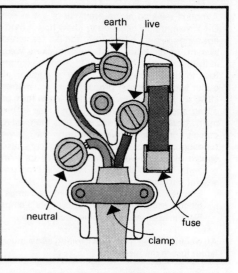

earth live
neutral
fuse
clamp

Rewiring a lamp holder

In theory the room switch should switch off the current to the holder, but it is possible for this switch to be wired up wrongly so that although the light goes out there could still be a live wire in the holder. It is therefore safest to switch off the current at the main switch. Then unscrew the cover, loosen the terminals and disconnect the flex. Press in the plungers to make sure the springs have not weakened. Thread the top cover over the flex, with about 20mm (¾in) of the ends bared and folded over. Tighten the cord grip if fitted.

Pass these ends through the terminals from opposite directions and tighten. Hook both wires round the plastic pillar. Then reassemble the holder.

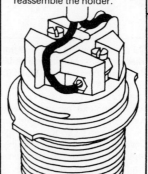

With an older type of brass holder, dismantle by unscrewing assembly ring and flex grip as shown.

Standard lamp holders usually screw on, and metal ones have an earth connection.

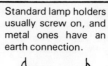

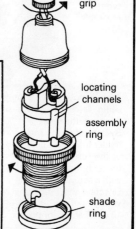

flex grip

locating channels

assembly ring

shade ring

Long flexes

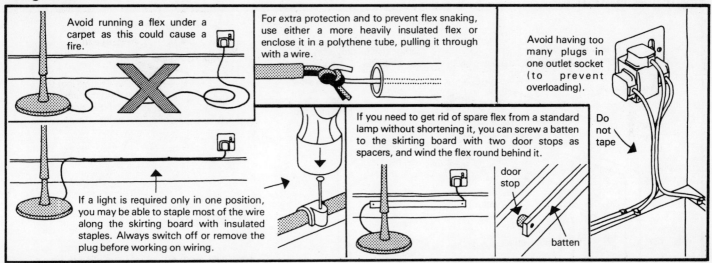

Avoid running a flex under a carpet as this could cause a fire.

For extra protection and to prevent flex snaking, use either a more heavily insulated flex or enclose it in a polythene tube, pulling it through with a wire.

Avoid having too many plugs in one outlet socket (to prevent overloading).

Do not tape

If a light is required only in one position, you may be able to staple most of the wire along the skirting board with insulated staples. Always switch off or remove the plug before working on wiring.

If you need to get rid of spare flex from a standard lamp without shortening it, you can screw a batten to the skirting board with two door stops as spacers, and wind the flex round behind it.

door stop

batten

Extension leads

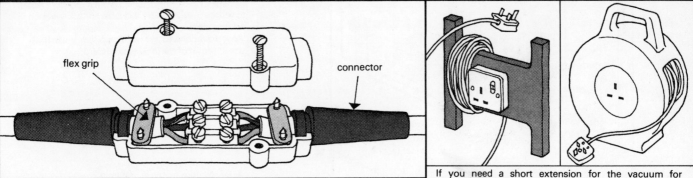

flex grip

connector

If you have to extend a flex connection, usually the best way is to rewire the equipment with a longer lead. (Whilst doing this make sure the rubber grommet which protects the wire where it enters a metal appliance is doing its job.) If this is difficult you can obtain a flex connector which is a safe way of connecting two wires.

If you need a short extension for the vacuum for instance you can wire one up using heavily insulated flexible cable and using a protected outlet socket, screwing the outlet socket to a board round which you can wind the wire.
You can however buy convenient extension leads which wind onto their own drums.

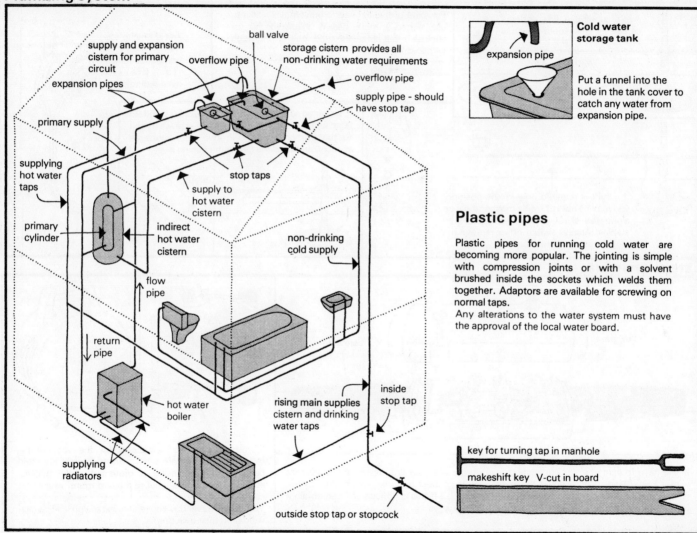

ball valve

supply and expansion cistern for primary circuit

overflow pipe

storage cistern provides all non-drinking water requirements

expansion pipes

overflow pipe

supply pipe - should have stop tap

primary supply

supplying hot water taps

stop taps

supply to hot water cistern

primary cylinder

indirect hot water cistern

non-drinking cold supply

flow pipe

return pipe

hot water boiler

rising main supplies cistern and drinking water taps

inside stop tap

supplying radiators

outside stop tap or stopcock

key for turning tap in manhole

makeshift key   V-cut in board

Cold water storage tank

expansion pipe

Put a funnel into the hole in the tank cover to catch any water from expansion pipe.

Plastic pipes

Plastic pipes for running cold water are becoming more popular. The jointing is simple with compression joints or with a solvent brushed inside the sockets which welds them together. Adaptors are available for screwing on normal taps.

Any alterations to the water system must have the approval of the local water board.

Turning off the water

The direct supply from the water mains usually leads only to the cold water tap in the kitchen and the storage tank. This storage tank, in the loft normally, feeds the other cold taps, lavatory cisterns, and so on. It also feeds the hot water tank which in turn supplies the hot taps.

There are usually two stop cocks or stop taps which turn off the main water supply—one in a trap outside the house (the property of the Water Board) and the other inside under the kitchen sink or in the cellar (the householder's responsibility). It is a sensible precaution to find out where these stopcocks are, to label them and check that they can be turned off by any member of the family. See diagram opposite. A key is needed for the outside stop cock.

If turning the main stop cock doesn't stop the leakage, the burst is on the outlet side of the storage tank. The water in the storage tank can be cut off by the outlet stop cock if one is fitted near the tank. (It is possible to stop the outlet by pushing in a rag on a broomstick, but this is not easy.) The simplest thing to do if no stop cock is fitted is to drain the storage tank by turning on all the cold taps and flushing lavatories, having turned off the main supply or tied up the float so that no more water enters the tank.

Important: remember that when the water tank empties there's no replenishment for the hot water tank. *Don't* run any hot water before turning off the water heater or putting out the fire, if you've a back boiler.

Burst pipes

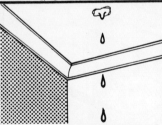

When water in a pipe freezes it expands nearly 10%, splitting the pipe but the split is not usually detected till the pipe thaws.

The first action to take when dealing with a flood from a burst pipe is to turn off the water supply (see above). Switch off all electricity in the area and do not turn on until wiring has thoroughly dried out.

If the ceiling is bulging, this can indicate a build-up of water above. Release this pressure by piercing the bulge with a skewer or other sharp instrument, allowing the water to flow through safely (place a container underneath).

Temporary pipe repairs

A makeshift repair is sometimes possible with a rubber pad and two car hose clips.

Here is a quick way or repairing a burst lead pipe (accepted by water board authorities only as a temporary repair). Tap the split part of the lead pipe together, and rasp or sand it clean.

Build up a bulge with one of the synthetic resin fillers made for general use. If you have a glass-fibre tape, this makes useful reinforcing.

You can thaw pipes out with a hot water bottle.

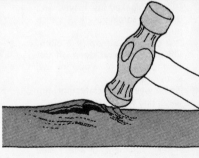

PLUMBING
Blocked waste pipes

Wastepipe blockages can cause great inconvenience but are usually fairly easy to clear. Most blockages in kitchen sinks are caused by a build-up of grease and solids. You can prevent this by occasionally pouring down a bucket of hot water, containing a handful of dissolved washing soda. This softens and removes the grease.

You will need:

force-cup ◄

rags

force-cup with metal shield to prevent turning inside out ▼

Larger force-cup is more effective.

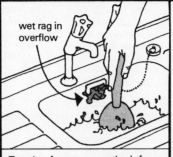

wet rag in overflow

Try the force-cup method for a start with about 25mm (1in) of water in the sink and making vigorous jerks up and down. A makeshift force-cup can be improvised with a bundle of rags. *N.B.* It will be necessary to block the overflow with a damp rag.

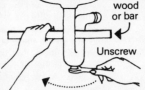

wood or bar

Unscrew

With a lead trap, hold the trap with a piece of wood or bar against the pressure while you unscrew the cap. Clear with flexible curtain wire or a suitably bent wire clothes hanger.

Copper traps and plastic traps can be unscrewed which makes cleaning easier. Always catch the water in a bucket underneath.

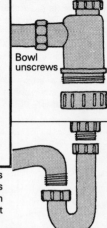

Bowl unscrews

For a lavatory pan, a large force-cup can be used vigorously but care must be taken not to damage the pan.

Blocked gulleys

1. Gulleys blocked by leaves and dirt stop drainage and cause puddles.
2. Bail out with a mop or a cloth. Lift out grate and clean off dirt with a piece of wood or old screwdriver.
3. Scrub well with disinfectant, hot water and washing soda.
4. Pump up and down with mop to clear blockage.
5. Use old spoon tied to a stick to remove sediment, or a tin nailed onto a stick.
6. If a washing machine drains into a gulley it is apt to deposit fluff (putting in a filter would avoid this) which can be removed with one or two nails driven through a stick.

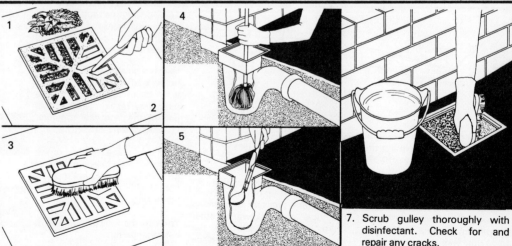

7. Scrub gulley thoroughly with disinfectant. Check for and repair any cracks.

Replacing a tap washer

Some water boards will replace tap washers free of charge; but since as a rule it is quite an easy job to tackle it is worth knowing how to set about it. You can get washers suitable for hot and cold taps, basin and bath taps. (There is a British Standards Institute specification for these washers.)

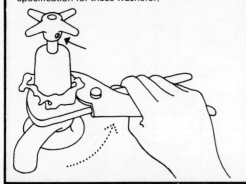

Unscrewing shield with slip-joint pliers.

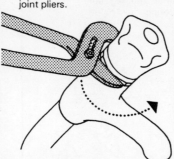

If you have this kind of tap, release the combined handle and shield by unscrewing nut as shown.

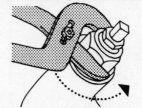

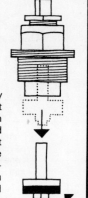

Unscrew the main body - you may need a fairly thin spanner of slip-joint pliers for this. Remove jumper (in some hot taps this is attached to head by a grub screw). Unscrew the nut holding the washer, change the washer and replace. Do not over-tighten the nut. Very occasionally you will find the tap seating is worn and the tap still leaks. A seating can be recut, but it is usually worth while replacing the tap.

Changing a Supatap washer

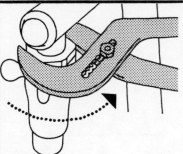

The main advantage of a Supatap is that a washer can be changed without turning off the water. For this reason they are used a good deal in local authority housing. Some authorities supply washers free of charge for tenants to do the job themselves. First unscrew the locking nut.

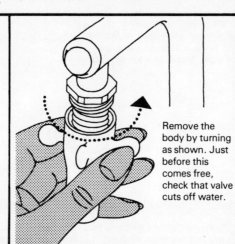

Remove the body by turning as shown. Just before this comes free, check that valve cuts off water.

Tap the protruding anti-splash device on a hard surface to loosen it and push it out. Pull out the jumper, which is pressed into the anti-splash device. Fit a complete new jumper which has a built-in washer.

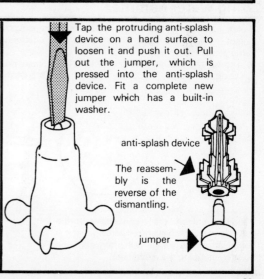

anti-splash device

The reassembly is the reverse of the dismantling.

jumper

PLUMBING
Repacking a tap spindle

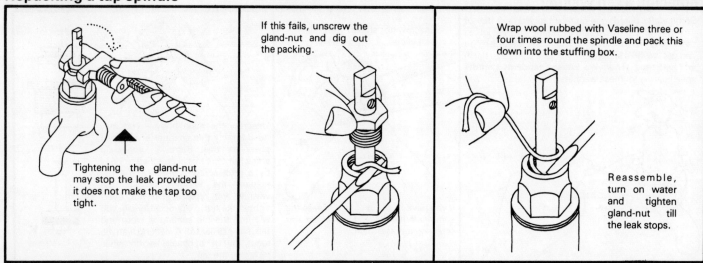

Tightening the gland-nut may stop the leak provided it does not make the tap too tight.

If this fails, unscrew the gland-nut and dig out the packing.

Wrap wool rubbed with Vaseline three or four times round the spindle and pack this down into the stuffing box.

Reassemble, turn on water and tighten gland-nut till the leak stops.

Curing water hammer

Water hammer is the noise—often quite violent—which you get when water is hammering inside a pipe. It is sometimes due to a loose tap washer (see instructions for replacing on page 23), sometimes to an unsuitable ball valve, sometimes to the chattering of the ball valve float in the cold water cistern, sometimes to a long length of unsupported pipe. First check for any loose tap washers.

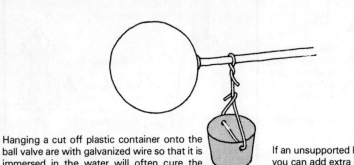

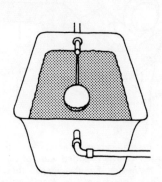

Hanging a cut off plastic container onto the ball valve are with galvanized wire so that it is immersed in the water will often cure the noise by damping the movement.

If an unsupported length of pipe is the cause, you can add extra supports. If in doubt, your water board will advise.

It is just possible that you will have to replace the ball valve for a more suitable type.

Overflowing lavatory cistern

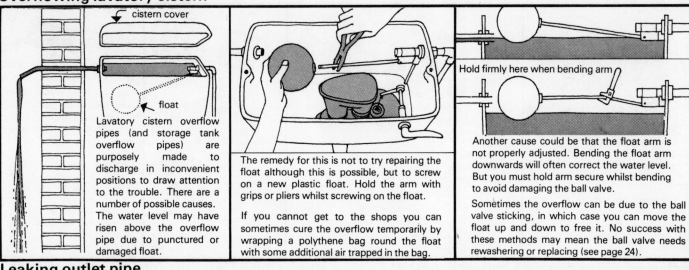

cistern cover

float

Lavatory cistern overflow pipes (and storage tank overflow pipes) are purposely made to discharge in inconvenient positions to draw attention to the trouble. There are a number of possible causes. The water level may have risen above the overflow pipe due to punctured or damaged float.

The remedy for this is not to try repairing the float although this is possible, but to screw on a new plastic float. Hold the arm with grips or pliers whilst screwing on the float.

If you cannot get to the shops you can sometimes cure the overflow temporarily by wrapping a polythene bag round the float with some additional air trapped in the bag.

Hold firmly here when bending arm

Another cause could be that the float arm is not properly adjusted. Bending the float arm downwards will often correct the water level. But you must hold arm secure whilst bending to avoid damaging the ball valve.

Sometimes the overflow can be due to the ball valve sticking, in which case you can move the float up and down to free it. No success with these methods may mean the ball valve needs rewashering or replacing (see page 24).

Leaking outlet pipe

New materials are available for repacking the outlet joint but this is usually regarded as a professional job. You can make a temporary repair which will probably last for years and years.
Wrap the joint with two or three layers of mastic tape.

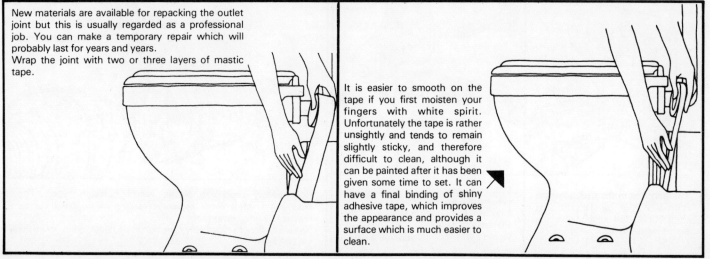

It is easier to smooth on the tape if you first moisten your fingers with white spirit. Unfortunately the tape is rather unsightly and tends to remain slightly sticky, and therefore difficult to clean, although it can be painted after it has been given some time to set. It can have a final binding of shiny adhesive tape, which improves the appearance and provides a surface which is much easier to clean.

PLUMBING
Replacing a Portsmouth type ball valve washer

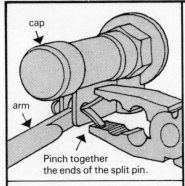

cap

arm

Pinch together the ends of the split pin.

A constant overflow could mean trouble with the float (see page 25) or it could be trouble with the ball valve which might be due to a faulty washer.

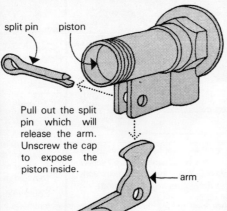

split pin   piston

arm

Pull out the split pin which will release the arm. Unscrew the cap to expose the piston inside.

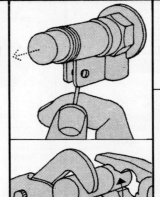

piston   cap

Next remove the piston. A sticking piston can be eased out with a nail or with the arm.

Unscrew end of piston. Protect with paper or rag (not shown) when gripping.

Replace washer as shown. Reassemble. Open split pin slightly.

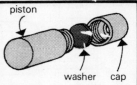

piston

washer   cap

Replacing a Croydon type ballcock washer

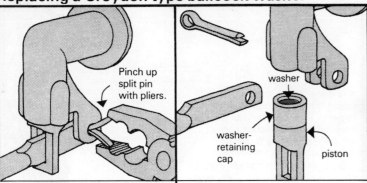

Pinch up split pin with pliers.

washer

washer-retaining cap

piston

The principle of the Croydon type ball valve is similar to the Portsmouth, but in this case the piston moves vertically.

Withdraw split pin and remove arm which will release piston.
Unscrew the piston cap as with the Portsmouth type.
Replace washer and reassemble.

Replacing a Garston type ball valve washer

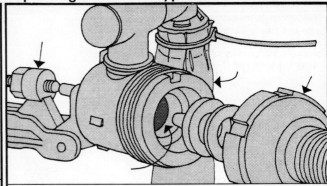

Now widely used are plastic valves (Garston type). The diaphram which replaces the washer rarely gives trouble. It can be reached by unscrewing cap.
Some equilibrium types now have miniature floats, quite unlike the old ball float.

Frost protection

See that the cold water cistern is well insulated. You can make your own box with 50mm (2in.) expanded polystyrene sheets held together with sticky tape or meat skewers, but kits are available for most tanks. You can also use glass fibre quilting. Do not insulate underneath the tank.

All exposed pipes should be lagged with glass fibre or rock wool bandage or split tubing (rigid expanded polystyrene or an approved flexible foam).

Glass fibre insulation can be pushed well into eaves to help eliminate draughts which make the loft colder. Lagging should be completed before the cold spell starts.

Salt in an external lavatory pan and cistern is a useful precaution if you are going away in winter.

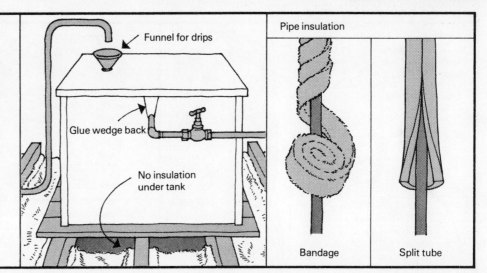

Funnel for drips

Glue wedge back

No insulation under tank

Pipe insulation

Bandage

Split tube

Locating heat losses

No two houses are the same and therefore do not have exact same heat losses—but the sort of losses that you are probably getting are shown here.

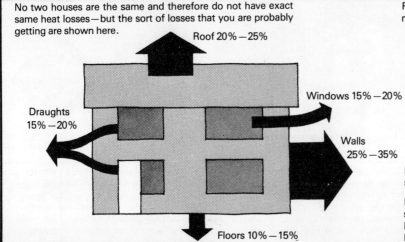

Roof 20%—25%

Windows 15%—20%

Draughts 15%—20%

Walls 25%—35%

Floors 10%—15%

Further advice and help on how to save energy in the home may be obtained by contacting:

Department of Energy, Thames House South, Millbank, London SW1P 4QJ

your coal merchant or solid fuel supplier, electricity or gas showroom

your local office of the Solid Fuel Advisory Service, or Living Fire Centres

National Home Improvement Centres (National Heating Council)

Home Heating Enquiry Line (Heating and Ventilating Contractors' Association), Coastal Chambers, 172 Buckingham Palace Road, London SW1W 9 TD

Most of the jobs necessary to improve the insulation are simple D.I.Y. jobs. See following pages.

Floor insulation is not so easy but if a floor has to be smoothed, substituting insulation board for hardboard will help—as will good carpet underlay. It is likely that doors will have to be cut down.

ENERGY SAVING
Lagging hot water tanks

An unlagged hot water tank could be wasting more than £1.00 per week. Make sure the jacket is at least 7.5 cm (3 in) thick. (An airing cupboard can often be made more effective by better ventilation).

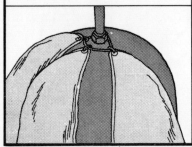

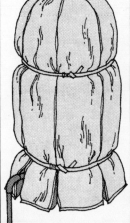

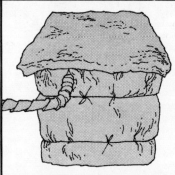

For square tanks use mineral wool or glass fibre quilting.

Expanded polystyrene sheets can be added outside.

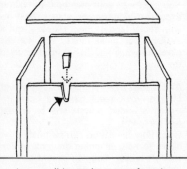

Inaccessible tanks can often be boxed in leaving the immersion heater and thermostat exposed. The box is then packed with Vermiculite.

Wise use of heat to reduce costs

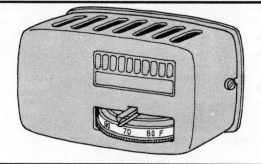

Lowering of central heating temperature or shortening the time it is on can make a considerable saving. Try to heat only those areas most in use using time switches where possible. Automatic door closers can be useful. Make sure the equipment is well maintained.

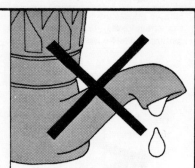

Switch off immersion heater if not used for long intervals or have a time switch fitted. Showers are much more economical than baths. One bath I have designed uses about ⅓ less water without loss of comfort.

Take care there are no dripping hot water taps and do not hem in hot water radiators.

Insulating the loft

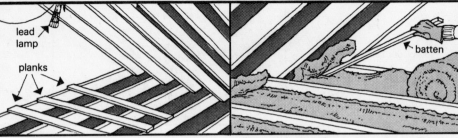

lead lamp

planks

batten

levelling Vermiculite with a spreader made from board

Pays for itself in 3-4 years.
Precaution: see that you have planks to walk on, positioned so that they do not overhang joists at ends, and a good light—preferably fixed.

Glass fibre or rock wool rolls should be at least 8cm (3in) thick. Some people find it is more comfortable to keep hands and arms bare and wash thoroughly to remove fibres—others prefer to wear gloves. Either way the fibre may be irritating but is accepted as not being harmful. Press rolls between joists starting at eaves where it helps to eliminate draughts.

Vermiculite
Pour in between joists and scrape to level at least 10cm (4in). Heap up over pipes. When the loft is insulated it will be colder so frost precautions are even more important (see p. 27). If you want to use the loft as a darkroom or hobbies room for instance, insulate under rafters with glass fibres and polythene under hardboard or plasterboard, with polyurathane backing. Expanded polystyrene ceiling tiles in lower rooms will help to insulate the loft, but are not thick enough on their own.

Insulating walls and windows

Pumping chemicals into the cavity forms an insulating foam and will show a considerable fuel saving but an expert check beforehand on any building defects is necessary and this work must be carried out by experts or serious trouble may result. Similar insulation is achieved by blowing in rock wool pellets.

Solid walls
Expense usually not justified but can be lined with plasterboard backed by expanded polyurethane.

Double glazing
The heat losses through windows can be halved by double glazing but as windows do not as a rule occupy a large part of the surface area the overall percentage gain is not so high as for instance with loft or cavity wall insulation.
Double glazing lessens the danger of condensation forming—an added advantage and can be useful for sound insulation (see p.33)

For new installations it is probably easiest to use 'sealed units'—units made to size of two sheets of glass (occasionally three) with a hermetically sealed airspace between. The units having the wider air space are more efficient.
Secondary glazing, that is secondary inner window allowing an air space of 2.5 cm (1 in) or more, is generally more efficient. There are many DIY kits for carrying this out. Heavy curtains can be quite a help. For existing units numerous kits are made to provide additional inner windows. These can usually be lifted out but the ease with which windows can be cleaned should be examined.

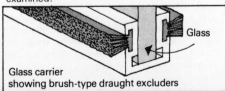

Glass

Glass carrier showing brush-type draught excluders

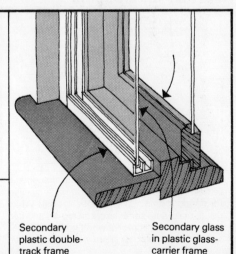

Secondary plastic double-track frame

Secondary glass in plastic glass-carrier frame

ENERGY SAVING
Curing draughts

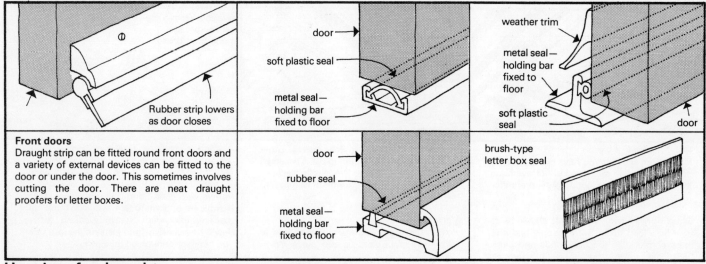

Rubber strip lowers as door closes

door
soft plastic seal
metal seal—holding bar fixed to floor

weather trim
metal seal—holding bar fixed to floor
soft plastic seal
door

Front doors
Draught strip can be fitted round front doors and a variety of external devices can be fitted to the door or under the door. This sometimes involves cutting the door. There are neat draught proofers for letter boxes.

door
rubber seal
metal seal—holding bar fixed to floor

brush-type letter box seal

Heat loss for draughts

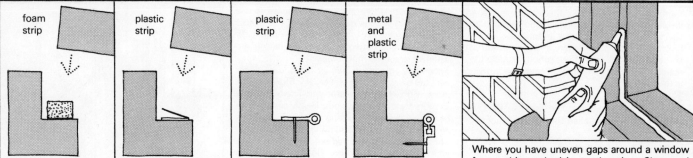

foam strip

plastic strip

plastic strip

metal and plastic strip

The easiest material to use to stop draughts is self adhesive foam strip which forms a cushion for the door or window to close against. When using, make sure surfaces are clean, dry and free from dust or the adhesive won't grip. This is not so neat or durable as more permanent plastic strips. One type becoming more popular has a built in siliconised brush 'pile' and this can be useful for sash windows. You can get details of a whole range of plastic and metal strips and draught proofing devices from the Weatherproofing Association.

Where you have uneven gaps around a window frame, this method is worth trying. Clean and sand the inside of the frame, then grease the window where it is going to touch. Squeeze a bath sealant on to the frame where there are gaps and leave this to set with the window closed. This will form a rubbery seal. Sealants are available in colours but a clear sealant will not look too unsightly on any colour.

Curing damp

The aim should of course not be just to obscure but to trace and deal with the cause of the damp. If it remains, there will always be a danger of fabric deterioration and rot. A damp patch above a chimney breast, for instance, is almost certainly due to condensation in the flue. If it is in a chimney which is not in use, see that the chimney is ventilated with a ventilation grille and, if possible, prevent moisture getting down the chimney by capping it. The problem is rather more serious when it arises with a slow-burning stove and it calls for chimney lining. A flexible liner is simplest.

Strip the wallpaper down to bare plaster and rub down with abrasive paper.

Stick on foil-backed, damp-resistant paper, or paint with a damp-resistant paint, or a heavy cement based water-proof coating. Whichever you choose may have to be suitable for applying on a damp surface and capable of being painted or papered over. If plaster is in poor condition, strip and paint onto cleaned bare wall. Follow instructions. it is

sometimes necessary to treat salts in brickwork with an anti efflorescence coating. Remember, surface coating does not cure the problem.

Treat as here

Always treat an area considerably larger than the patch that shows.

For severe dampness such as in a basement more drastic methods may be necessary: plastering over corrugated lath or forming an inner skin with an airspace.

Where a cure is very difficult, an inner lining may be necessary—plaster or a patent corrugated material or rot proofed battens, a layer of polythene and plasterboard with a vapour-proof barrier.

Outside
Do not tackle roof work without the correct scaffolding and roof ladder. If uncertain, employ a builder for roof work. Don't take risks!

Chimney flaunching (cement covering round pot). Renew with PVA adhesive added to cement mortar, or fill cracks with a mastic. Broken hopper head—see gutter repairs page 36.

Damp proof course replacement
Generally professional job involving brick removal or dripping in damp-repelling liquid to form a barrier or by the electro-osmosis process.

Concrete floor
There are preparations which can be painted over. Avoid using vinyl tiles if damp. A concrete floor should of course have a damp proof membrane sandwiched in it.

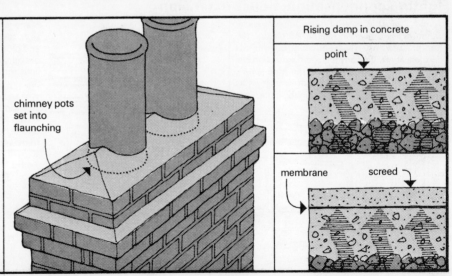

chimney pots set into flaunching

Rising damp in concrete

point

membrane   screed

PROOFING
Fighting condensation: kitchen

Condensation is caused by a warm, damp atmosphere meeting a cold surface and can be cured in two ways.

1. By continually replacing the air in room with colder, less humid air, i.e. providing better ventilation. Air vents often help, but cannot be relied upon. An extractor fan is best, but get advice on the size you need for your room. Try to get the air moving over all moisture-producing units, such as the cooker and sink.

2. By insulating particularly cold surfaces. In extreme cases it could be worth covering a particularly exposed wall with plasterboard having an insulated backing. There are anti-condensation paints which improve the situation when the condition is not severe.

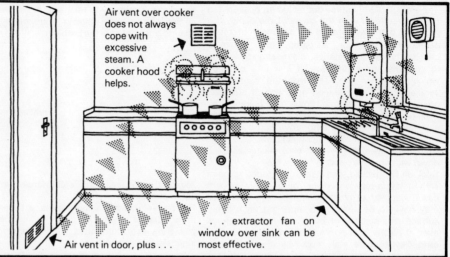

Air vent over cooker does not always cope with excessive steam. A cooker hood helps.

Air vent in door, plus . . .

. . . extractor fan on window over sink can be most effective.

Fighting condensation: house extension

Avoid anything that produces water vapour - like a paraffin heater. An electric fan heater can greatly reduce problems of condensation. If poorly insulated extension has been added to a room where the atmosphere may be moist, provide as much ventilation as you can, both in the room and in the extension.

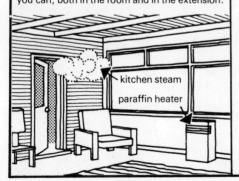

kitchen steam

paraffin heater

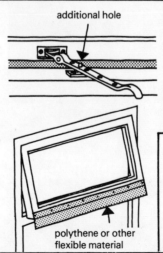

additional hole

polythene or other flexible material

Many windows fitted to extension rooms open rather wide and produce draughts. With an ordinary window stay you can limit the degree of opening by drilling an additional hole, or you can fit a stay with closer adjustment. You can also lessen the direct draught by tacking an apron of polythene to the outside of the window.

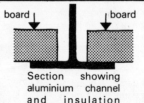

board

board

Section showing aluminium channel and insulation boards.

You can fit a suspended ceiling of insulation board in aluminium channel, as air trapped above boards improves insulation and lessens condensation. If you need light through the ceiling you can fit a second layer of transparent plastic sheeting, leaving an air gap. An anti-static preparation (normally sold for keeping light fittings free from dust) will help distribute condensation if rubbed on the plastic sections. Wiping with detergent sometimes helps.

Wet rot Due to persistant damp, timber goes dark brown to black; brittle where dry, spongy when wet. The first sign is often paint peeling or cracking. Does not spread like dry rot.

Remedy Replace with timber treated with fungicidal preservative. A water repellent preservative is useful for external timber. Eliminate damp.

Dry rot Must not be neglected as it can spread fast, attacking new timber, even crossing masonry and steelwork. It is due to excessive dampness in timber usually where ventilation is bad, arising from plumbing faults or damp proof course failure.

Remedy Ruthlessly cut out all affected timber and about 900mm (3 ft) beyond and burn. Treat surrounding timber with dry rot fluid. Strip plaster in area. Wire brush infected brickwork. Further infection may have to be treated with dry rot fluid. Paint new joist ends with a bituminous paint and coat surrounding area with fungicidal fluid. Rerender where necessary with special impregnated plaster.

Most important Remove cause of dampness and provide good ventilation.

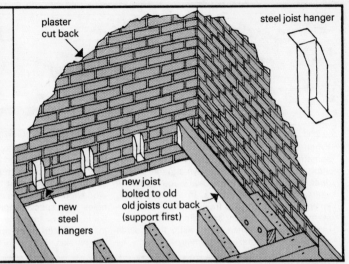

plaster cut back

steel joist hanger

new steel hangers

new joist bolted to old old joists cut back (support first)

Soundproofing

To prevent sound coming through, you need a heavy dense material, or an unbroken air space. Acoustic tiles make a room seem quieter because they absorb some of the noise in that room. A bad wall can often be improved by making sure the window and door frames are well fitted, and by a heavy coat of plaster or cement. In extreme cases you can build an additional breeze block wall with an air space between this and the original wall. Special thin lead sheet can also be used, but the result of all this effort can be disappointing because noise can enter through gaps, round windows and doors, through any opened window or a chimney, voids above and below the walls or through other air leaks. An understanding with the neighbours is often the only solution. If you live near an airport you can get a soundproofing grant.

Sound penetrates ceiling and door . . .

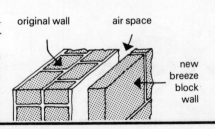

. . . acoustic tiles (above) and padding (left) reduce noise level, but do little to prevent sound penetration.

original wall   air space

new breeze block wall

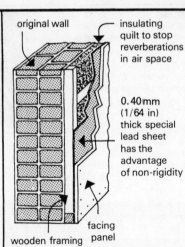

original wall

insulating quilt to stop reverberations in air space

0.40mm (1/64 in) thick special lead sheet has the advantage of non-rigidity

wooden framing   facing panel

When used for sound insulation double glazing must have at least 120mm (5in) between panes and should be lined with a sound-deadening material for maximum efficiency.

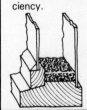

PESTS
Woodworm

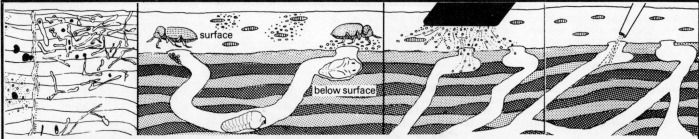

surface

below surface

When treating for woodworm it helps to know something of the life cycle of the pest. From June to August the female lays eggs in cracks, open joints and bore holes. Lava stage lasts three years. Here damage occurs. In summer beetle emerges, often flying to fresh timber. New cycle starts. Treatments vary according to where the beetle is found. When floor joists, floorboards and lath and plaster wall framing are badly infected some timber may be so weak that it has to be cut out and replaced and the remaining timber may need specialist treatment. Vacuum well in spring to remove dust and eggs. Saturate with woodworm insecticide using brush or injecting in holes with special applicator. **Warning**: Some liquids are inflammable for one week, especially in unventilated areas, and is harmful if inhaled or left on skin. Eyes also need protection. Woodworm is frequently found in the loft and here it can be treated by standing a Flytox block (renewed every year for three years) in the loft. The vapour this gives off kills the woodworms, but is harmless to human beings. Furniture in the house can be treated rather laboriously by this method, again, extended over three years.

Pests

Crawling insects Beetles, cockroaches, silver fish, spiders, woodlice, are liable to appear at any time of the year. Ants in July and August, beetles April to September, ground beetles June to August, and earwigs May to October.

Silverfish - flat and silvery, harmless but sometimes damage paper and fabric found in damp dark places under carpets, skirtings etc, nocturnal so you can search with a torch.

Flying insects The direct aerosol spray is effective but the slow release evaporator containing Dichlorvos in all its forms sprayed into grilles, blocks, etc, is a convenient and lasting method. The vapour needed for this purpose is quite harmless to humans.

Biting insects Use a safe insect repellent contained in cream in a tube, lotion in a bottle, a spray, or introduced recently, tissues impregnated with liquids. For sensitive skin, choose a product which is suitable.

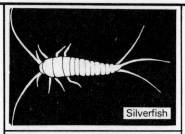

Silverfish

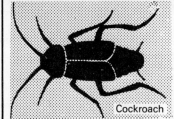

Cockroach

Prompt disposal of waste food preferably in tied up bin liners is a protection against insects. (Products are now available which deal with a wide variety of insects so exact identification is not always necessary.)

Contact the local authority if in serious trouble with household pests - they will usually help without charge.

Preparation for outside painting

First, choose a dry, wind-free day to tackle the job, when everything has had time to dry out. Dampness can cause peeling, very hot sun can lead to blistering. You may feel like doing that part of the job which you can reach easily from a board on two step ladders, but if you have a reasonable head for heights, and you hire safe equipment, a two-storey house should not be too difficult. Choose a ladder which is not too heavy and extends at least three rungs above the gutter. Do-it-yourself tower scaffolding provides a less tiring platform. If you have a hard, level base, a paved area for instance, and scaffold on locking wheels, you can move it without dismantling. It should be secured by tying to the house near the top if more than 4M (14ft) high. Do not lean a ladder against the scaffold.
The foot of the ladder should be about ¼ of the ladder height away from the house.

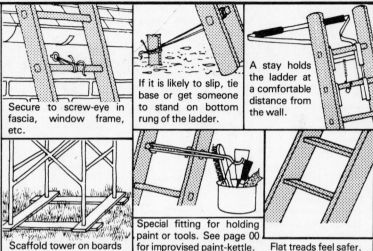

Secure to screw-eye in fascia, window frame, etc.

Scaffold tower on boards

If it is likely to slip, tie base or get someone to stand on bottom rung of the ladder.

A stay holds the ladder at a comfortable distance from the wall.

Special fitting for holding paint or tools. See page 00 for improvised paint-kettle.

Flat treads feel safer.

Plan the job carefully. Make sure you have enough materials and the right tools. Check and repair gutters, pointing and window putty. Use stiff, dry brush on stone paint. If you have to burn off paint, beware of fire, particularly when working under the eaves. All surfaces should be dusted with a brush. A tack rag to which dust sticks is useful for cleaning sanded surfaces. Stir paint thoroughly (except for non-drip preparations) and strain it through a stocking if the tin was opened some time previously. Special hand stirrers are available, and there are stirrers for use with electric drills. For stonework there is a wide choice of paint, including cement paint and newer materials containing mica, sand, nylon fibre or rubber. You may have to use a sealing compound before applying paint over old paint of a different kind—your paint supplier will advise you. Anti-fungus preparations may be used where necessary.

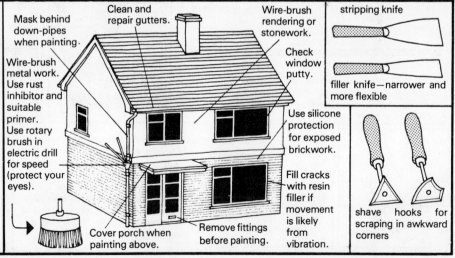

Mask behind down-pipes when painting.

Wire-brush metal work. Use rust inhibitor and suitable primer. Use rotary brush in electric drill for speed (protect your eyes).

Clean and repair gutters.

Wire-brush rendering or stonework.

Check window putty.

Use silicone protection for exposed brickwork.

Fill cracks with resin filler if movement is likely from vibration.

Cover porch when painting above.

Remove fittings before painting.

stripping knife

filler knife—narrower and more flexible

shave hooks for scraping in awkward corners

OUTSIDE JOBS
Repointing brickwork

Dog for raking out.

Club hammer and cold chisel for use where mortar is too hard.

Hawk: screw and glue a dowel to 230mm (9in) square 12mm (½in) thick board.

First, rake out the joints. If you have an electric drill, there is an inexpensive bit (a router) which works quickly.

Mix up the mortar with three parts of soft sand to one of cement, preferably masonry cement, so that it is fairly stiff and smooth. Put a little onto the hawk and pick up with the trowel as shown in the drawing. You can buy an additive for making it spread more smoothly.

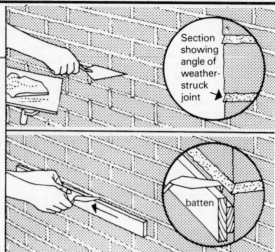

Section showing angle of weather-struck joint

batten

For the usual weather-struck joint use a small pointing trowel to smooth in, first the vertical joints, then the horizontal joints. To finish the lower edges neatly cut them off with a miniature trowel with the end bent over. Next run trowel along a batten held about 12mm (½in) away from the wall by spacer blocks nailed on. Finally, brush off all loose mortar with a soft brush.

batten with blocks ➡

Leaking gutters

Generally one thinks about gutter repairs in winter, but the time to tackle them is when the weather is good.

spirit level — batten

gutter

A long batten and spirit level will show up sagging or slope in the wrong direction. Adjust by repositioning the existing brackets or by screwing extra ones to the fascia or by wedging with packing.

Unscrew bolt

Repack joint

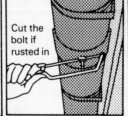

Cut the bolt if rusted in

Squeeze

rubber seal

union clip

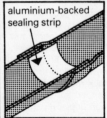

aluminium-backed sealing strip

To cure a leaking cast-iron joint unscrew the bolt with a screwdriver, holding the nut with a spanner, and repack with mastic putty. You may have to cut off the bolt and fit a new one. To repair a hole, clean well inside and out. Stick thick cardboard round the outside, fill the hole with a glass fibre and resin repair kit, and remove the cardboard.

Squeeze plastic gutter to break joint to renew rubber seals. (Petrol will remove perished rubber.) New parts should be from the same make of guttering. For an easy and usually effective way to deal with most leaks, wire-brush and clean inside thoroughly; then press down self-adhesive heavy-duty aluminium sealing strip on the inside and add a strip on the outside. You can use this sealing material for many sealing jobs, even on porous surfaces, provided you use a special sealer.

Broken stone step

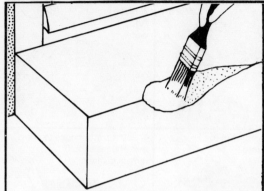

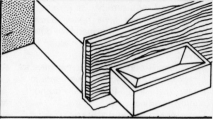

A stone step with a broken edge can be dangerous. Wire-brush damaged part and paint with a PVA adhesive.

Mix a little PVA adhesive into cement mortar.

Wedge a board against the front of the step with a sheet of polythene to prevent mortar sticking (see above, right).

Trowel mortar into space and smooth off. A synthetic resin stone repairing compound provides a durable repair but is more expensive.

Slippery outside steps

Treat the steps with self-adhesive, non-slip nylon strips (which can also be used on wood, metal or cement) using a special primer for preparing rough or porous surfaces. First, remove grease, wire-brush and prime (if necessary), then press on strips. Or, after wire-brushing steps, you can put on a coat of general purpose adhesive and sprinkle sand over this before it dries (areas not to be sanded should be masked with tape). When dry, brush off surplus. sand. After steps have been used a few times, repeat the process. Painted white or any other light colour, the steps will be easier to see and less hazardous.

Wire brush the steps and press on self-adhesive strips.

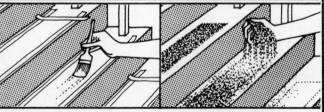

Alternative method: paint with adhesive and sprinkle on sand.

OUTSIDE JOBS
Concreting paths and drives

Tools and equipment: tape measure string pegs spirit level heavy hammer battening spade wheelbarrow bucket watering can possibly steel or wood float trowel

For extensive concreting you may have to check on any restrictive covernants in a lease, or with the local authority surveyors office.

Concrete mixes and storage
Concrete mixes (measured by volume)

For paths and thin sections Preferably one part cement, two parts sand, three parts coarse aggregate. With this mix seven bags of cement will produce one cubic metre of concrete.

Or one part cement, three and a half parts ballast (which is all in aggregate).

For drives, foundations and heavy duty work Preferably one part cement, two and a half parts sand, four parts coarse aggregate. With this mix seven bags of cement will produce one cubic metre of concrete.

Or one part cement, three and a half parts ballast.

For bedding mortar
One part cement, three parts coarse sand.

Method Turn the dry mix over till thoroughly mixed then form hollow, spray on water and continue turning over till you can just squeeze a little water out of a handful.

Avoid concreting in frosty weather.

Storing Store cement in dry place clear of floor with newest bags underneath. Store outside (only if necessary) on platform well covered by polythene. With part used bags inside plastic bags. Sand and aggregate on hard surface or tarpaulin.

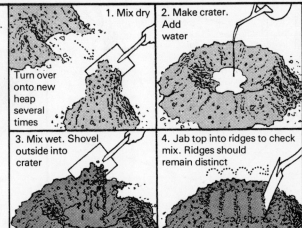

1. Mix dry
Turn over onto new heap several times

2. Make crater. Add water

3. Mix wet. Shovel outside into crater

4. Jab top into ridges to check mix. Ridges should remain distinct

Laying concrete

Preparation
Mark out area using a set square or T square or for extensive work a made up square. Dig out very soft earth, grass and roots. Allow depth for concrete and hardcore combined. 50mm (2in) for paths and 100mm (4in) for drives.

A slight fall 25mm (1in) to 100mm (4in) in the right direction is helpful to shed rainwater but should be even. Set up for a true level and measure down on the pegs. A hose, particularly a transparent one, can be used for levelling. Fill with water and cork ends. Top up if necessary.

For soft earth a 25mm (1in) to 50mm (2in) layer of rubble rammed down hard with a baulk of timber with a well rolled layer of sand on top.

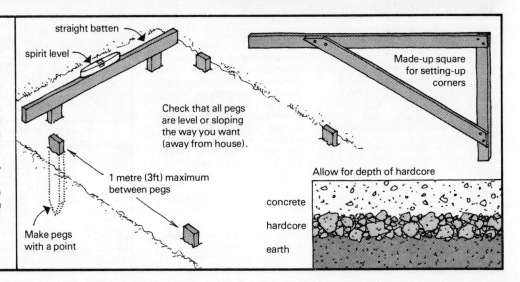

straight batten

spirit level

Made-up square for setting-up corners

Check that all pegs are level or sloping the way you want (away from house).

1 metre (3ft) maximum between pegs

Make pegs with a point

Allow for depth of hardcore

concrete

hardcore

earth

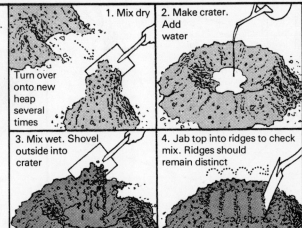

Laying concrete

Framework That is the frame to contain the concrete. Use 25mm (1in) sawn timber, 50mm (2in) for a drive. Support this with pegs on the outside. Nail by hammering against something solid and divide into sections of 1.5-2 metres (4-6ft) with removable cross-piece.

When concreting a slab against a wall lay this in alternate sections. Keep concrete 15cm (6in) below damp proof course.

Laying concrete Tip into framework from barrow. Drag it level then tamp down with batten.

It can be left with this rough finish or smoothed with a wooden float. Too smooth will make path slippery when wet. A stiff brush across concrete gives non-slip brush finish.

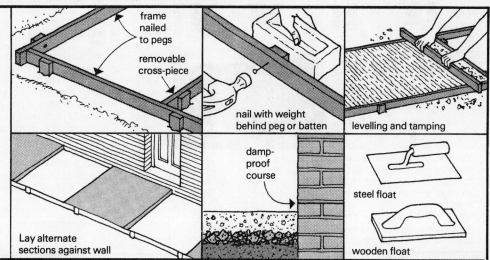

frame nailed to pegs

removable cross-piece

nail with weight behind peg or batten

levelling and tamping

Lay alternate sections against wall

damp-proof course

steel float

wooden float

Crazy paving and concrete paving stones

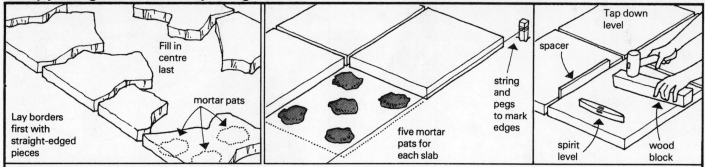

Fill in centre last

Lay borders first with straight-edged pieces

mortar pats

five mortar pats for each slab

string and pegs to mark edges

Tap down level

spacer

spirit level

wood block

Broken paving is sometimes available from the local authority. Break up and select so that gaps are not too wide and the edges are straight for border. For light use, can be laid dry on well compacted layer of sand.

Two or three mortar pats underneath makes it easier to tap down to level with a mallet. Do not roll.

Concrete paving stones Can be dry laid on sand or tapped down to level with mortar pats. Use 6mm ($\frac{1}{4}$in) batten to get even spacing. Tap down level with surrounding blocks and check for horizontal.

When set joints can be filled and then raked out with rounded batten about 6mm ($\frac{1}{4}$in) below surface.

You can make patterns with stones of different colours and sizes.

Plan on paper before ordering.

For decorative finish, bed cobble stones into cement over concrete base already set.

OUTSIDE JOBS
Resurfacing a path or drive

Fill in pot-holes and roll.

Apply weedkiller

Pierce bag, tip out and rake smooth.

There is a Macadam compostion which can be laid cold; and it can be used with coloured chippings so that it harmonizes with the surroundings. All you need for laying this is a rake, a stiff broom, a garden roller (as heavy as possible) and a watering-can.

Remove all weeds and grass and apply a weedkiller. Fill in any potholes with Macadam compound and roll. Clear any dust and loose material. For some surfaces you may have to brush on a coating of primer made for the purpose and leave it to set. (Ask the supplier's advice about this, if in doubt.) Wash the broom. Empty out the compound or pierce the bag and rake it out to avoid unnecessary lifting, and spread it on to a thickness of about 20mm (¾in). Roll it out evenly keeping the roller wet. After a few days, give the surface another roll. Scatter in the decorative chippings and, after a final roll, you should have an attractive, transformed area.

Making a garden pool

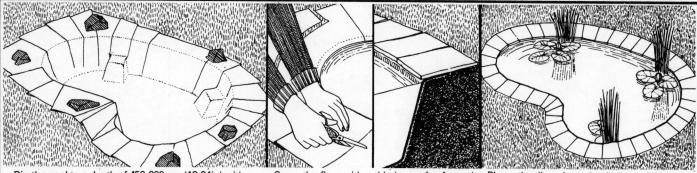

Dig the pool to a depth of 450-600mm (18-24in) with sloping sides. You may like to arrange shelves which will provide a platform for water lilies and rushes. Make these 200-300mm (8-12in) square and level them off at about 230mm (9in) below the surface.

Cover the floor with a thin layer of soft sand or sifted soil. For lining the pool you can buy a moulded fibre-glass tray, but the cheapest is thick polythene sheeting in black, blue, or natural colour (you must use it doubled), or PVC-coated Terylene.

Place the liner into the hollow, folding it where necessary so that it makes a good fit, and leaving about 6in (150mm) overlapping around the edges. Temporarily weigh down this overlap with stones. Fill the pool with water, and then fit slightly projecting edging slabs all round the edge of the pool.

Repairs to corrugated plastic roofs

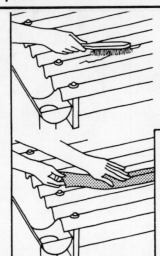

A mastic sealing tape or an aluminium-backed mastic tape, particularly the heavy-duty type, should make a good repair. This will not look very tidy from below and will not be absolutely permanent, but it can be a quick way of overcoming an inconvenient leak. Strips are available in various widths. A primer gives better adhesion with porous surfaces like brickwork or concrete. Fairly dry conditions are an advantage, and if it is cold the material should be warmed a little before use.

First, clean and wire-brush the surface around the crack, then smooth the sealing strip on by hand or with a decorating roller.

These sealing strips can also be used for repairing and sealing joints in gutters and down-pipes, replacing flashings, and sealing greenhouse glazing bars.

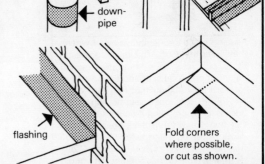

glazing bars

down-pipe

flashing

Fold corners where possible, or cut as shown.

Repairs to a greenhouse

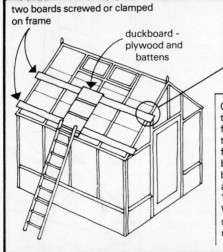

two boards screwed or clamped on frame

duckboard - plywood and battens

G-clamp or screw

One of the main problems is reaching the roof to replace glass or to paint the frames. One way of doing this is to fix two boards across by screwing on and filling the screw holes afterwards, or by using G clamps. Then make a duck board (plywood with battens tacked across) to hook over the top board. You can reach this with a small ladder. Warning - if the cross battens are not securely fixed a nasty accident could result.

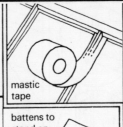

mastic tape

battens to stand on

batten to hook over board

Horticultural glass is cheaper than ordinary glass. This should be bedded in putty on a dry day (having first primed the timber) but you may find it worthwhile to cover all the bars with mastic tape (tape with a resinous base) in which case you need not worry about the putty over the glass. This is a simple way of dealing with leaks. There are compounds which help you to get rid of the algae between the panes - algae does no harm but it may block a little light. If some timbers have rotted away, you can build them up with a resin-repair compound, having first scraped the wood very carefully. If the rot is extensive they will have to be replaced.

OUTSIDE JOBS
Mending rotting fence posts

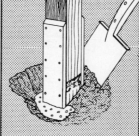

Fencing posts frequently rot away where they enter the earth. The ideal repair is to fit a concrete spur, but this means bolting it on. A quicker and easier way is to dig a hole 300-450mm (12-18in) deep all round the post, supporting it if necessary by propping it up with a spade. Cut two 40mm (1½in) thick boards to the width of the post and twice the depth of the hole—if the hole is 300mm (12in) deep, make the boards 600mm (2ft) long.

Chamfer the top of each board so that it slopes gently, and when fitted will allow rain to run off easily.
Use preservative on all boards before use, but don't use creosote if the post is very close to plants. It may harm them; safe preservatives are available.

Using non-rusting nails, nail the boards so that they support the two accessible sides of the post, right down to the bottom of the hole.
Strengthen the other two sides of the post similarly. Ram in stones and earth.

Two other useful repairs: when the top of a post is rotting, tack on a small roof of zinc or aluminium backed sealing tape. One method of sealing end-grain timber against water penetration is to paint it with synthetic resin adhesive. Where the fence is coming away from the posts in places, try using rust-proofed angle repair plates.

Mending sagging gates and posts

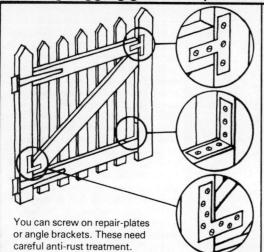

You can screw on repair-plates or angle brackets. These need careful anti-rust treatment.

For a more attractive appearance pin and glue on waterproof plywood offcuts. Roughen the gate's surface first with the end of a rasp. Use waterproof glue and pins. Annular ringed pins — see below — are useful.

You can sometimes force the joints apart sufficiently without dismantling the gate to insert a synthetic resin or other waterproof adhesive. Hinges can sometimes be moved so that the screws are in new positions. If a screw has seized in, try cutting it with a hacksaw. Non-rusting screws put in with grease or candlewax will be an advantage.
For tightening screws which are loose in their holes, remove the screw and ram in some asbestos fibre plugging compound.

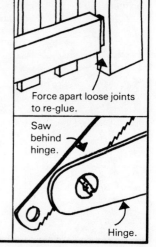

Force apart loose joints to re-glue.

Saw behind hinge.

Hinge.

Labour-saving kitchens

If you are a busy housewife at home with a family, you are likely in a year to be walking further than from here to Moscow - entirely in the kitchen. So it is well worth looking at the kitchen to see if you can rearrange it in any way to eliminate any unnecessary movements. It is of course difficult to achieve the ideal, since the kitchen may be poorly designed to start with and some of the fittings may already be there, but some alterations may be possible. Here is a suggestion for a kitchen where movement has been cut to a minimum - minimum stooping, reaching and walking. The solution must be worked out for each individual kitchen.

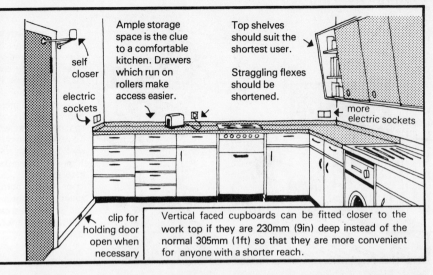

self closer

electric sockets

Ample storage space is the clue to a comfortable kitchen. Drawers which run on rollers make access easier.

Top shelves should suit the shortest user.

Straggling flexes should be shortened.

more electric sockets

clip for holding door open when necessary

Vertical faced cupboards can be fitted closer to the work top if they are 230mm (9in) deep instead of the normal 305mm (1ft) so that they are more convenient for anyone with a shorter reach.

Bathroom planning

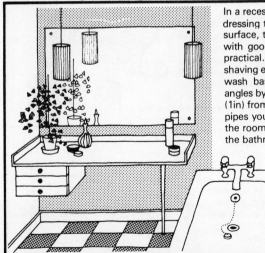

In a recess or corner of a bathroom it is easy to build an attractive dressing table unit. You can buy shelves with a laminated plastic surface, the edges covered with edging strips. Fit a mirror behind with good mirror lighting . . . double shades are attractive and practical. Drawers provide valuable storage for cosmetics or shaving equipment. You can also build a complete unit around the wash basin. Horizontal plumbing will be obscured from most angles by a vertical board about 100mm (4in) deep set back 25mm (1in) from the front edge of the shelf. If you have unsightly vertical pipes you can build a cupboard underneath to obscure them but the room will look slightly smaller. If you have no hot water tank the bathroom is often a good place to build an electrically heated airing cupboard which will also give you piping hot towels. Great care must be taken with any electrical apparatus in a bathroom. There must be no possibility whatever of touching any exposed wires or elements. If you are fitting a new bath it will look more luxurious and be more functional if you take the feet off, stand the bath on the floor, fitting wedges to stop the bath rocking, and sinking the waste trap under the floor boards.

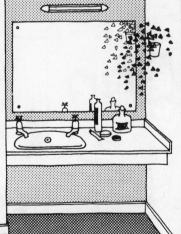

The ideas shown left include: pin-up board of 12mm (½in) insulation board, rough cork tiles with edges trimmed with coloured tape; moulding on the wall round the bed, inset with fabric or vinyl paper to give a sitting-room atmosphere - even with the current preference for mattresses on the floor, instant shelving to create storage space and interest.

To make a record storage area on a suitable shelf or cabinet top (as shown right), cut a 10mm (⅜in) thick plywood panel and attach it to the wall with screw-eyes and elastic loops—shock cord from a boating shop is suitable. Suggest some unusual decorations: coloured candles, old flash bulbs or polystyrene packing cases can spark off ideas.

Large, comfortable floor cushions can be easily and quickly made from foam chips or polystyrene beads.

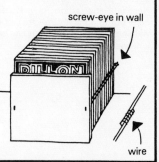

screw-eye in wall

wire

Posters may be stuck on to hardboard and hung in bold groups to harmonize with the furniture. Smaller pictures can be stuck on to 12mm (½in) chipboard offcuts with edges taped with coloured tape—stick the tape flush with the picture surface, folding it underneath if it is wider than 12mm (½in). A polyurethane-finished veneered chipboard top can convert two white-wood chests to a large desk. A removable board for model-making can protect the top. Fit the board against the wall or with a batten underneath the front edge which locates against the edge of the desk. A box seat with lifting lids can give extra storage space. It can be mounted on castors to push under the bed. Try rush mat squares on the wall as a back-rest. Chair and table can be made from a cut-down barrel.

Reglazing a wooden window

Remove the broken glass and putty using a rag or glove or, best of all, leather gardening gloves. An old chisel or a pointed knife will do the job, but a hacking knife is made for the job: tap it round the opening with a hammer. Pull out the brads which hold the glass in, scrape all round and paint the bare wood with a paint primer. Measure the exact size to fit the glass in and deduct 3mm (⅛in) from both dimensions to allow a clearance. Order the glass to this size. Try the glass in the frame when you get it back.

Knead the putty into a ball, adding a little linseed oil if it is too stiff. With the thumb and forefinger, press the bedding putty into the frame then press the glass firmly into the putty till you have squeezed this to about 3mm (⅛in).

Tap the brads into the frame to hold the glass in position. Space them about 230mm (9in) apart, making them flush with the glass and use the

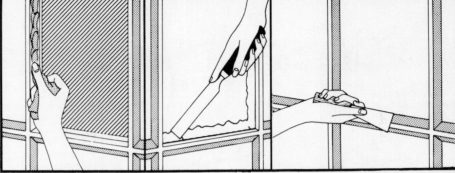

side of an old flat-sided chisel to tap them in, sliding this in contact with the glass.

Now press the facing putty around the glass, and smooth out at an angle with a putty knife or scraper. Always remember to hold the knife at a constant angle and try to make a neat mitre at the corner (see below). A special tool which is made for this job makes it much easier. Cut away the excess putty on the inside of the window, and brush with a soft paint brush to make a perfect seal. Don't paint for a week or so.

Reglazing a metal-frame window

Hack out the broken glass in the usual way, using gloves for safety.

Remove the glazing clips and note their positions. Scrape and wire-brush the frame and paint with a rust inhibitor.

Then, as above, thumb in the bedding putty made specially for metal frames.

Get the glass cut 3mm (⅛in) smaller than the two dimensions for the frame opening. Press the glass into the bedding putty, replace the clips and thumb round the facing putty.

Bevel neatly with a putty knife held at a constant angle with a firm, even pressure, mitring the corners and working towards the centre.

Cut away all excess putty and brush with a soft paint brush. Leave for at least a week before painting.

mitre

metal frame

bedding putty

glass

clip

facing putty

INSIDE JOBS
How to renew a broken sash cord

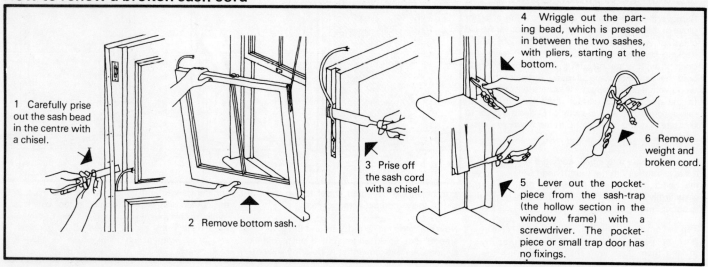

1 Carefully prise out the sash bead in the centre with a chisel.

2 Remove bottom sash.

3 Prise off the sash cord with a chisel.

4 Wriggle out the parting bead, which is pressed in between the two sashes, with pliers, starting at the bottom.

5 Lever out the pocket-piece from the sash-trap (the hollow section in the window frame) with a screwdriver. The pocket-piece or small trap door has no fixings.

6 Remove weight and broken cord.

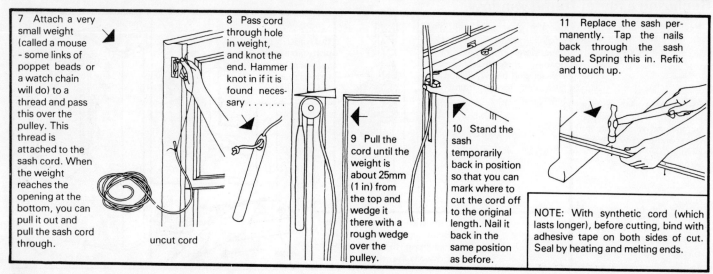

7 Attach a very small weight (called a mouse – some links of poppet beads or a watch chain will do) to a thread and pass this over the pulley. This thread is attached to the sash cord. When the weight reaches the opening at the bottom, you can pull it out and pull the sash cord through.

uncut cord

8 Pass cord through hole in weight, and knot the end. Hammer knot in if it is found necessary . . . .

9 Pull the cord until the weight is about 25mm (1 in) from the top and wedge it there with a rough wedge over the pulley.

10 Stand the sash temporarily back in position so that you can mark where to cut the cord off to the original length. Nail it back in the same position as before.

11 Replace the sash permanently. Tap the nails back through the sash bead. Spring this in. Refix and touch up.

NOTE: With synthetic cord (which lasts longer), before cutting, bind with adhesive tape on both sides of cut. Seal by heating and melting ends.

Tiling a splashback

The splashback can be of laminated plastic, plastic-coated hardboard or easy-to-fix ceramic tiles. First, sandpaper the surface of the wall to make sure it is clean and free from dust. Paint if not removed should be scratched and roughened.

You will need some of your tiles with one rounded edge, known as R1, and some with two rounded edges, R2. The splashback illustrated requires a total of eighteen tiles made up of eight ordinary, eight R1s and two R2s.

If there is a gap between the washbasin and the wall, fill this with mastic, which can be bought in tubes. Mark the

R2	R1	R1	R1	R1	R2
R1					R1
R1					R1

centre of the top edge of the washbasin and start tiling left and right of this.

Use five blobs of tile adhesive on the back of each or comb a thin layer onto the wall.

Most tiles are separated by small lugs to ensure regular spacing. When the adhesive has set, squeeze grouting material into the spaces between the tiles and wipe off any surplus. Any gap between the tiles and the top of the

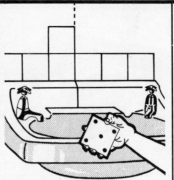

washbasin can be covered with plastic or ceramic beading.

When tiling a larger area if you are starting from a base which is not roughly horizontal, take a light batten to the wall to rest

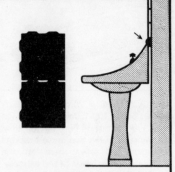

the first row of tiles on and when the rest of the tiling has set, remove the batten and cut the lower tiles to fit. Measure first so that you get an equal margin on each side.

Filling a gap between a bath or sink

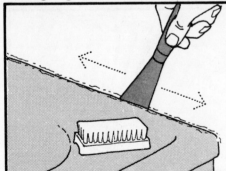

Modern fillers are now available which can be pressed in and smoothed out easily. They remain semi-flexible to take up

any further movement that takes place.
Scrape and clean out the gap thoroughly. Wipe dry.

Squeeze in a silicone rubber sealing compound which you can smooth with a wet finger. Cut the tube nozzle to a suitable size.

All these methods can of course be used for filling other similar gaps, e.g. between wall tiles and the door frame.

INSIDE JOBS
Fitting a pelmet and curtain rail

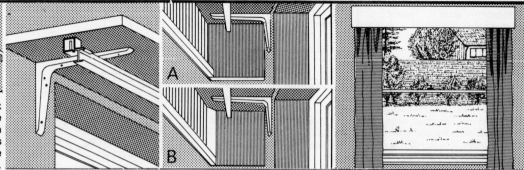

You will need a 25mm (1in) thick pelmet board 100-150mm (4-6in) wide and 100-150mm (4-6in) longer than the window. Take two angle brackets and plug and screw them into the wall, one on each side of the window, so that the tops of the brackets are just above the window frame. Rest the board on the brackets and mark the positions of the screws. Then remove the board and drill pilot holes on the marks.

Screw the curtain-track onto the board, keeping the supports clear of the bracket holes. Choose your own depth of pelmet: for a guide, 25mm (1in) of pelmet for every 300mm (foot) of the height of the curtain will give it a well-proportioned appearance. Now screw the board to the brackets.

For the pelmet front you have a choice of fitting methods. **A** Pin and glue on the wooden ends (the same type of board as the pelmet board), and for the front use hardboard with a thin batten 12-20mm ($\frac{1}{2}$-$\frac{3}{4}$in) as a stiffener along the bottom. **B** Use moulded hardboard pinned and glued to the top and secured at the front-and-side joint with a 12mm ($\frac{1}{2}$in) glue block (triangular shaped wood). Glue into the angle.

Fitting curtains with no pelmet

It depends on the room and your own taste whether curtains go across the top of the window or extend up to the ceiling. For window (and ceiling) fitting, drill holes for screws and fix batten above window frame projecting about 230mm (9 in) on each side.

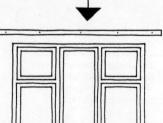

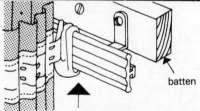

batten

You can choose from a variety of attractive front-fitting tracks. Then screw on to batten.

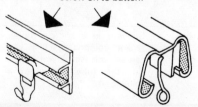

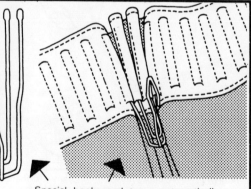

Special hooks and tapes automatically pleat curtains. Depending on the thickness of curtain fabric, allow for an amount one and a half times or double the width of the window.

Making drawers run smoothly

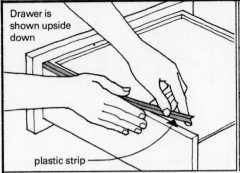

Drawer is shown upside down

plastic strip

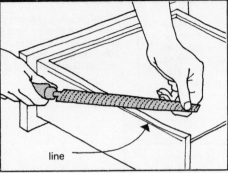

line

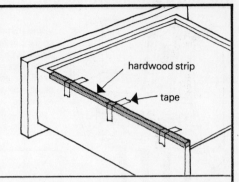

hardwood strip

tape

If cabinet slides are rough, sandpapering and rubbing with candle wax will often cure the problem. If space permits, stick 6mm ($\frac{1}{4}$in) plastic angle strip along drawer slides with impact adhesive.

Where drawer has worn badly, renew slides with hardwood strips.
With drawer upside down, draw a line to the depth of new strip and rasp down.
Stick on new strips using synthetic resin adhesive. Hold in place with sticky tape until

adhesive has set, or fix with panel pins, driving these below the surface. Rub all sliding parts with candle wax. The drawer will slide so much more easily that there may be a tendency to pull it right out. A drawer stop is the answer here (see below).

Preventing drawers pulling out

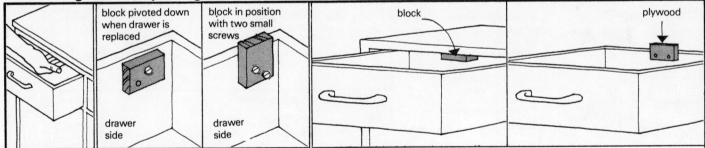

block pivoted down when drawer is replaced

block in position with two small screws

drawer side

drawer side

block

plywood

If, when you put your hand inside the drawer opening, you can feel a projecting batten above the drawer, you can use this as a stop.
Take the drawer out and, about 75mm (3in) from the back, screw a block on to the drawer side so that the block projects about 12mm ($\frac{1}{2}$in) above the side. Pivot the block down to replace the drawer. Then pivot the block up and put in a

second screw with the drawer in position
Where there is no projecting batten, it may be sufficient if the block catches on to the drawer above.
If, when you feel inside the drawer-opening, there is a smooth surface above the drawer, you can, with the drawer in position, fix a block to stop the drawer sliding out. Fixing the block with

screws can be difficult. Instead, roughen the two surfaces and use an impact adhesive.
If the back of the drawer is not high enough to catch against the block, screw on a raised piece of plywood.

INSIDE JOBS
Making a simple wall rack

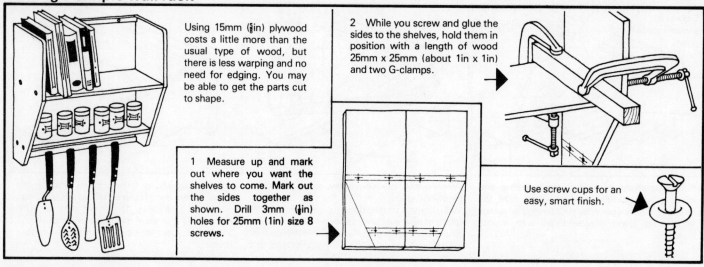

Using 15mm (⅝in) plywood costs a little more than the usual type of wood, but there is less warping and no need for edging. You may be able to get the parts cut to shape.

1 Measure up and mark out where you want the shelves to come. Mark out the sides together as shown. Drill 3mm (⅛in) holes for 25mm (1in) size 8 screws.

2 While you screw and glue the sides to the shelves, hold them in position with a length of wood 25mm x 25mm (about 1in x 1in) and two G-clamps.

Use screw cups for an easy, smart finish.

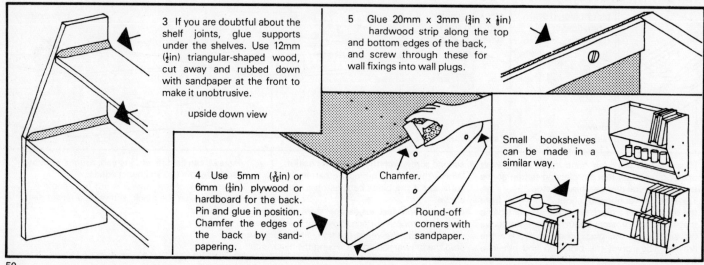

3 If you are doubtful about the shelf joints, glue supports under the shelves. Use 12mm (½in) triangular-shaped wood, cut away and rubbed down with sandpaper at the front to make it unobtrusive.

upside down view

4 Use 5mm (³⁄₁₆in) or 6mm (¼in) plywood or hardboard for the back. Pin and glue in position. Chamfer the edges of the back by sand-papering.

5 Glue 20mm x 3mm (¾in x ⅛in) hardwood strip along the top and bottom edges of the back, and screw through these for wall fixings into wall plugs.

Chamfer.

Round-off corners with sandpaper.

Small bookshelves can be made in a similar way.

Fitting shelves into a recess

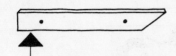

1 Measure up from floor and mark positions of undersides of shelves allowing room for books. Bearers will support shelves underneath each end. Make an adjustment if the floor is badly out of level.

2 Cut wall bearers from 20mm x 40mm (¾in x 1½in) wood, drilling two 5mm (³⁄₁₆in) holes for 45mm (1¾in) size 10 screws. Hold the bearers in position and mark through the front holes the position for the wall plugs.

3 Fix plugs. Fix the front screw on each bearer. If floor slopes badly fit shelves horizontally using spirit level. Place shelf on top, adjusting bearers until shelf is level. Mark position for second hole, fit wall plug, and screw bearers tight.

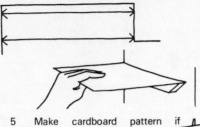

4 Measure recess front and back.

5 Make cardboard pattern if necessary to fit irregularities.

viewed from underneath

6 Cut shelves to fit irregularities. If shelves need extra support fit stiffeners underneath. You can glue shelves to bearers with synthetic resin adhesive, weighting shelves till set. 20mm (¾in) chipboard veneered in various woods or covered in laminated plastic makes ideal shelving.

7 If you are left with any awkward gaps, cover these with small quarter-round beading.

Fitting a shelf on metal brackets

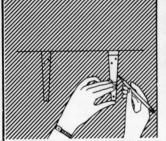

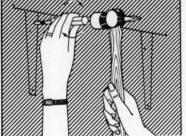

The main worry when fitting a shelf is whether or not you can make it absolutely secure. The section on wall fixings (page 7) should help you to do this. Make sure you pinpoint the holes for the screws accurately. First draw a line where the shelf has to go,

using a spirit level (a device with an air bubble in liquid to make sure the lines are horizontal). If it is a small spirit level stand it on a batten and draw a line along this. Mark the positions of the wall brackets as shown above.

Make a hole for the plug using either a jumper bit (a hardened steel tool made specially for the job), turning it as you hammer in, or a masonry bit fitted to a hand or electric drill. So long as the shelf is not too heavy, and the plaster in your wall is of average thickness, you will need a 40mm (1½in) size 8 screw, a 40mm (1½in) size 8 plug, and a number 8 jumper or masonry bit. Remember to put sticky tape around the jumper or drill bit at the depth you need to sink the plug below the surface.

See page 7 for fixing instructions. If you intend to paint the brackets, do it before fixing.

Stand the shelf on top and mark fixing holes. Make pilot holes with a small drill or a bradawl, and screw on the shelf, making sure that your screws are not too long.

THINGS TO MAKE
Picture framing in passe-partout

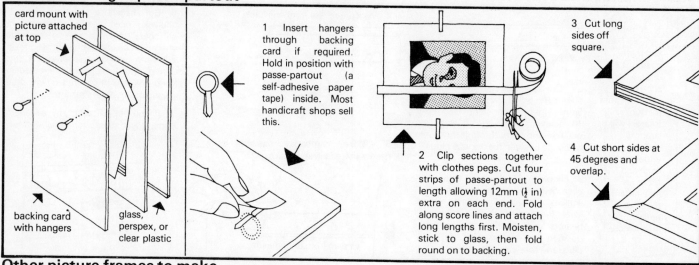

card mount with picture attached at top

backing card with hangers

glass, perspex, or clear plastic

1 Insert hangers through backing card if required. Hold in position with passe-partout (a self-adhesive paper tape) inside. Most handicraft shops sell this.

2 Clip sections together with clothes pegs. Cut four strips of passe-partout to length allowing 12mm ($\frac{1}{2}$ in) extra on each end. Fold along score lines and attach long lengths first. Moisten, stick to glass, then fold round on to backing.

3 Cut long sides off square.

4 Cut short sides at 45 degrees and overlap.

Other picture frames to make

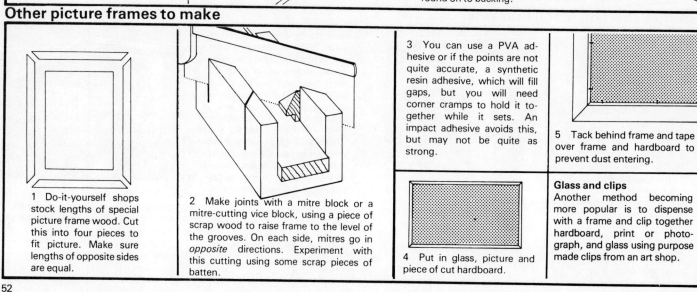

1 Do-it-yourself shops stock lengths of special picture frame wood. Cut this into four pieces to fit picture. Make sure lengths of opposite sides are equal.

2 Make joints with a mitre block or a mitre-cutting vice block, using a piece of scrap wood to raise frame to the level of the grooves. On each side, mitres go in *opposite* directions. Experiment with this cutting using some scrap pieces of batten.

3 You can use a PVA adhesive or if the points are not quite accurate, a synthetic resin adhesive, which will fill gaps, but you will need corner cramps to hold it together while it sets. An impact adhesive avoids this, but may not be quite as strong.

4 Put in glass, picture and piece of cut hardboard.

5 Tack behind frame and tape over frame and hardboard to prevent dust entering.

Glass and clips
Another method becoming more popular is to dispense with a frame and clip together hardboard, print or photograph, and glass using purpose made clips from an art shop.

Fixing mirrors

To save money on a mirror where perfect reflection is not required buy sheet mirror cut to size. Take off the sharp edges by rubbing lightly with a knife-sharpening stone. Then edge the mirror with a strip of self-adhesive wood veneer. This can be fixed with the usual corner fixings.

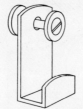

Alternatively you can buy mirrors in a variety of sizes with the edges already ground. These are easily fixed with the sliding clips provided, which can of course be used on other mirrors.

Screw lower clips to wall. Stand mirror on them and mark top corners.

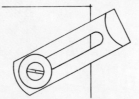

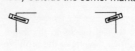

Screw top clips to wall so that they swing freely outside the corner marks.

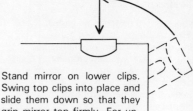

Stand mirror on lower clips. Swing top clips into place and slide them down so that they grip mirror top firmly. For un-even walls add packing washers behind the clips to bring the mirror away from the wall.

Drawer space saver

You nearly always need more storage space in a kitchen, but for many objects drawers are too deep and if you fill them right up, you can't get at anything. One suggestion is to fit a sliding tray. When you push this to the back of the drawer you can easily reach the lower section.

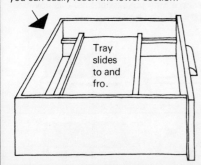

Tray slides to and fro.

Carefully mark the positions for the battens 12mm x 12mm ($\frac{1}{2}$ in x $\frac{1}{2}$ in) (which act as slides) about 75mm (3 in) from the top of the drawer.

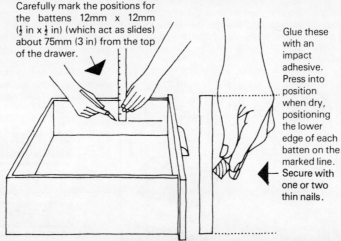

Glue these with an impact adhesive. Press into position when dry, positioning the lower edge of each batten on the marked line. Secure with one or two thin nails.

Glue similar battens along the front and back edges of a piece of 6mm ($\frac{1}{4}$ in) plywood, cut to a clearance fit. With a plastic tray on top, of suitable size, you will have increased your drawer capacity considerably – and you can still reach everything.

HOUSEHOLD REPAIRS
Repairing broken china

The best glue to use for a strong, waterproof repair to glass and china is an epoxy resin. You buy this in two tubes - one is glue, the other hardener.

Squeeze the recommended amounts out of the two tubes and thoroughly mix together so that the glue will set properly. Then make sure the joins are clean. Usually, with a clean break, there is no need to touch the pieces at all.

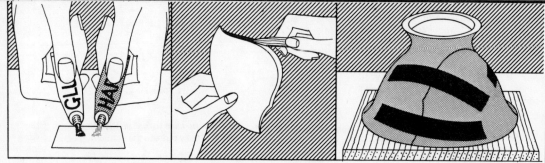

Spread the adhesive on to both surfaces and press them together so that they fit snugly. Then wipe off any surplus before it sets with a damp rag. If the object has broken into lots of pieces, you may have to stick some of the smaller pieces to the larger ones first and allow to set. You now have the problem of holding the pieces together till the adhesive sets. For this, plastic sticky tape which is slightly stretchy can be most useful. Stick the tape on so that it holds the pieces together. In some cases a piece of cardboard taped on as a sort of splint, can be a help.

A warm room will speed up the setting time of the adhesive, but ideally you should wait about four days before putting the repaired article back into service. You can buy an epoxy adhesive that sets in five minutes, which makes hand holding possible. It is still advisable not to put the article back into service for some time.

Carpet repairs

For most repairs you need a rubber latex adhesive specially made for carpets. Apply to both surfaces, wait until nearly dry, then press together. Cigarette burn: wind a thread taken from the edge of the carpet or wool of the same colour round a large knitting needle so that when it is bunched up it fits into the hole with loops projecting. Stick into the hole with latex, wait until dry, then cut off the loops to the level of the pile.

Larger holes: cut a piece of carpet to fit the hole - take some from where it won't be noticed. Match direction of pile by running finger through it and stick in the patch with carpet underneath. This tape can be used for joining any two pieces of carpet together.

Edging a carpet. Axminster: pull off a few rows of thread leaving a projecting fringe. Fold this fringe underneath and stick it to the underside of the carpet. Wilton: stick plastic-faced carpet tape underneath the edge leaving a little projecting. Fold this upwards: stick to edge of pile. Keep tape below surface.

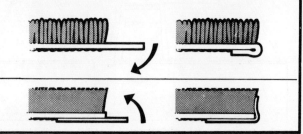

Descaling a kettle

Scaling is a nuisance, it wastes fuel and it also makes boiling slower so it is worth removing. Use a descaling agent with care and do not let it come into contact with eyes, skin or fabric. Pour the recommended amount into the kettle, half-filled with water, and wait until the solution stops effervescing and the scale has disappeared. You may have to add a little more descaling liquid if scale remains.

If badly furred, boil until almost dry.

Tap out loose scale and proceed as above.

Boil and rinse *thoroughly*.

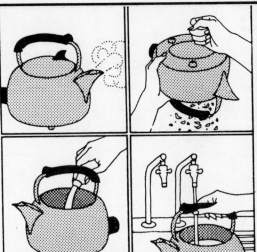

Applying a non-stick finish to a saucepan

First remove all grease with steel wool and detergent. Then spray on the non-stick finish. Stand the pan upside-down and cook it in the oven for 30 minutes at 200°F, 93°C or Mark ¼. This will not give you a factory finish, but you can reclaim any old pan effectively. This method cannot be used on pans with wooden or plastic handles - unless the handles can be removed. The spray is inflammable and should be kept away from naked flames. Remember, also, that no aerosol can should ever be punctured.

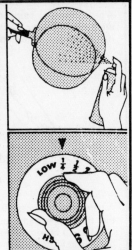

Repairing split leg and castor

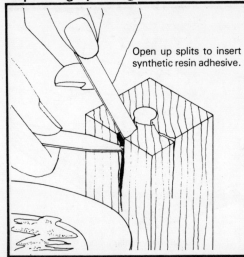

Open up splits to insert synthetic resin adhesive.

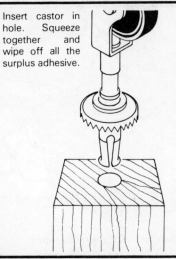

Insert castor in hole. Squeeze together and wipe off all the surplus adhesive.

Wrap polythene round leg to prevent adhesive sticking to string. Bind tightly with string. Leave for two or three hours in a warm atmosphere. If this is not effective you can bind the leg with fibre glass tape stuck with synthetic resin or smear a synthetic resin containing a filler onto the leg, bind tightly with string and smooth the resin over the top of the string. When it is set paint in a suitable colour.

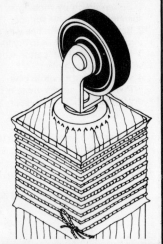

HOUSEHOLD REPAIRS
Stripping pine furniture

A proprietary paint stripper is probably the easiest method. It is advisable to follow the manufacturer's instructions and wear rubber gloves, as the stripper may need neutralizing.

A hard finish may need light roughening or scratching first so that the stripper can penetrate. Sandpaper first or in extreme cases use a broken hacksaw blade as shown, with the grain, but be careful not to cause permanent scoring.

Finally rub down thoroughly before finishing. Polyurethane varnish gives a tough finish. Apply at least two coats, rubbing in the first with a soft rag and rubbing down between coats with fine wire wool (grade 000). For a satin finish use fine wire wool then wax on top of the final coat.

Removing heat or water stains from a French-polished surface

1 Soften polish by rubbing in methylated spirit sparingly on the table surface.
2 Remove polish with fine wire wool. Do not go through to stain. Allow to dry for several hours.
3 Make up pad of cotton-wool wadding and soak with button polish.
4 Wrap the pad in cotton cloth.
5 Polish with circular motion (right). Allow to dry for half an hour and repeat.

Warning: take great care if the table is a valuable piece of furniture. Try the method out on an unobtrusive spot.

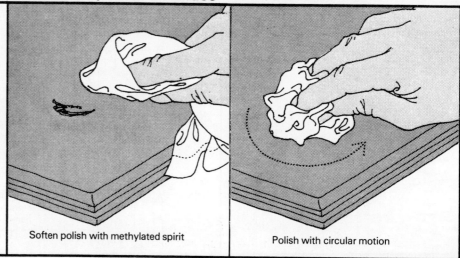

Soften polish with methylated spirit

Polish with circular motion

Fitting Pirelli webbing to a chair seat

Pirelli webbing is a rubberised webbing which has some resilience so that a seat cushion of minimum thickness can be used.

1 Remove old webbing if fitted. Tack 50mm (2in) rubber webbing with 15mm (⅝in) improved tacks about 12mm (½in) from frame edge, avoiding old tack holes.

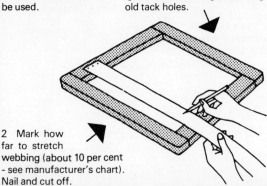

2 Mark how far to stretch webbing (about 10 per cent - see manufacturer's chart). Nail and cut off.

3 Keep gaps between to less than width of webbing. Make sure webbing has even tension.

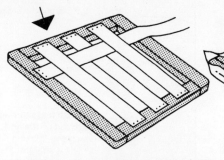

4 Make seat cushion using plastic foam. Depth of cushion for dining-room chair: 40-50mm (1½-2in); for easy chair: 70-100mm. Stick calico strips along top edges.

5 Tack four sides of cover compressing foam slightly.

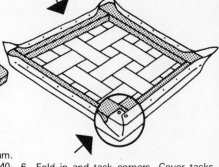

6 Fold in and tack corners. Cover tacks with gimp and gimp pins, obtainable from hardware shops.

Renewing the webbing of a coil-spring chair

Even if only one strap has broken, it is usually worth renewing all the webbing. Remove hessian covering and then remove webbing with an old chisel or plastic-handled screwdriver. Ease out tacks. Cut the twine attaching the springs to the webbing. Fold one end of new webbing over about 20mm (¾in) and tack in position with four tacks, avoiding old holes.

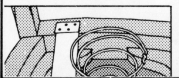

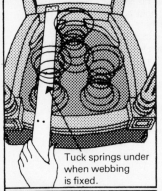

Tuck springs under when webbing is fixed.

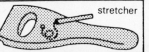

stretcher

To tighten the webbing, wrap it round the ends of a small block of wood about 200mm (8in) long and then clip a fold of webbing against the side of the chair. Adjust the webbing so that, when you lever the block downwards it stretches it tight. You can buy a stretcher that works on the same principle and is made for this job. A loop of webbing passes through a hole in it and is secured with a wooden pin.

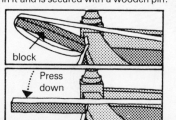

block

Press down

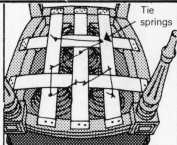

Tie springs

Put two tacks through one thickness and then cut off webbing so that you can fold over 20mm (¾in) and add more tacks. A curved upholstery needle helps when tying the springs to the webbing. Replace hessian cover, or, if you feel this gets too dirty, use a plastic fabric that can 'breathe'.

HOUSEHOLD REPAIRS
Replacing canvas on a deckchair

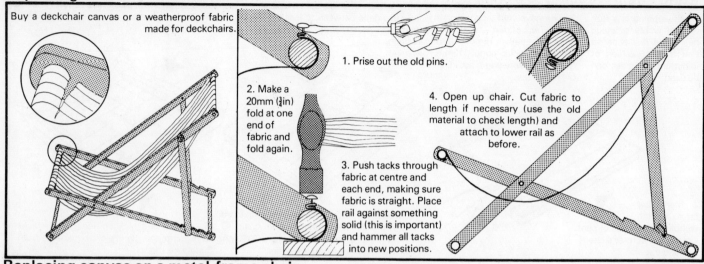

Buy a deckchair canvas or a weatherproof fabric made for deckchairs.

1. Prise out the old pins.

2. Make a 20mm (¾in) fold at one end of fabric and fold again.

3. Push tacks through fabric at centre and each end, making sure fabric is straight. Place rail against something solid (this is important) and hammer all tacks into new positions.

4. Open up chair. Cut fabric to length if necessary (use the old material to check length) and attach to lower rail as before.

Replacing canvas on a metal-frame chair

Buy a new canvas or a length of plastic deck-chair fabric to replace the original fabric: be certain to allow suffi-cient for wrapping it round the tubes, allow-ing for 20mm (¾in) fold (use old material to measure the length).

Cut off old fabric. Make a 20mm (¾in) fold at end of new fabric: wrap new fabric round tubes, starting at the top. With a large darning needle and 60-gauge matching thread or (tougher still) white Terylene binding thread from a boat shop, back-stitch fabric round tubes, following old line of stitching. A sail-maker's thimble might help.

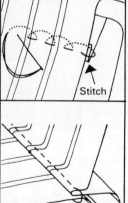

Stitch

Stitch

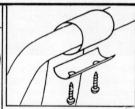

If fabric was attached with gutter-shaped pieces of metal, un-screw these to remove fabric. Wrap new fabric round once and replace gutters. You may need a Pozidrive screwdriver (with a cruciform head).

Sharpening knives, scissors, shears etc

There are several patent sharpeners but knives and penknives can be effectively sharpened on an oilstone or with a slipstone.

The same applies to scissors. Keep the angle the same as before. Blades should have a slight curve. Screw may need tightening.

Sharpening shears is a similar operation but sharpening can be started with a very fine file. Sharpen an axe with a fine file or a slipstone.

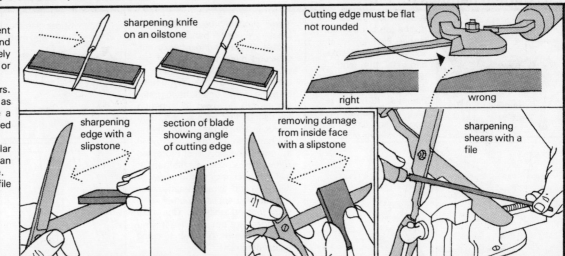

sharpening knife on an oilstone

Cutting edge must be flat not rounded

right   wrong

sharpening edge with a slipstone

section of blade showing angle of cutting edge

removing damage from inside face with a slipstone

sharpening shears with a file

New handles for old

First measure the depth with a pencil and mark this on the handle as shown, right.

Put thumb against end of handle . . .

. . . and mark depth.

If you have a vice, hold the handle in this while you shape it using whatever tool you have for shaping – a rasp, a nutmeg grater-type shaper, a plane or even a sharp knife.

Shaper trims handle end to size. Continue rasping and shaping until the handle can be pressed almost to the depth of the pencil mark.

Coat the shaped end with adhesive preferably a gap-filling synthetic resin. Rub the inside of the hole with sandpaper and (left) ram the head on by tapping the handle on a hard floor. Fix with a long screw, or hammer in a nail, holding the head on something solid (if on a bench, over one of the bench legs). Then the handle should never fall out.

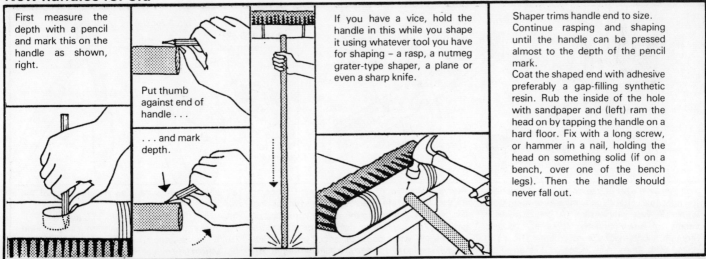

GARDEN JOBS
New garden handles for old

Remove screw

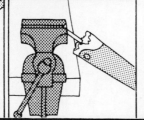

large screw at least 5cm (2in) long

A softwood handle will do the job but ash lasts longer. First remove the screw and the broken end. If the end is jammed, grip it in a vice and tap the rake with a hammer. If no broken end projects, put in a good-sized screw and hold this in the vice.

It will probably be necessary to taper the new handle to the socket. Put the handle beside the rake and mark the length of the taper. Then guess the diameter of the end and mark this. If you have no plane, a rasp or a nutmeg grater shaper can be used for tapering the handle: first square it off, then round it. Pinch the socket round the handle in a vice, and screw in a round-headed, rust-protected screw. Drill a pilot hole first, about half the thickness of the screw to help it in and avoid damage. This method also applies to other tools with tapered sockets. One rake reminder—try not to leave it lying points upwards because it could be dangerous.

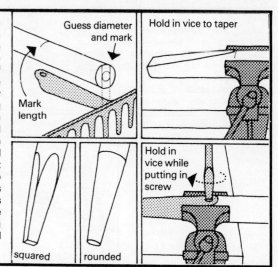

Guess diameter and mark

Mark length

Hold in vice to taper

squared

rounded

Hold in vice while putting in screw

Garden tool storage

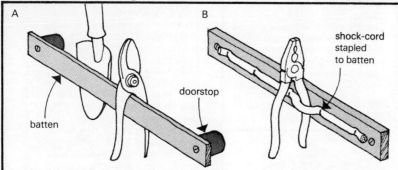

A

batten

doorstop

B

shock-cord stapled to batten

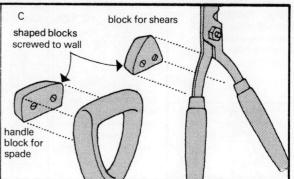

C

shaped blocks screwed to wall

block for shears

handle block for spade

You can save a lot of gardening time if you have the right tools stored ready in racks or hung from hooks. A very simple rack (A) which takes a variety of small trowels, forks and cutters requires a batten of 25mm x 12mm (1in x ½in) drilled with 4mm ($\frac{3}{16}$in) holes at 300mm (12in) intervals. Small door stops form good spacers. All you have to do is screw up the batten and door stops together into the wall of your shed or garage. You can make useful clips to secure small tools with loops of shock cord (thick elastic) stapled to a batten at a suitable height (B).

Simply push their handles into the grip of the rubber.
Improvise fittings as shown in C above.
For the equipment you want to carry around (such as secateurs, gloves, labels, wire) a household tidy makes a useful carrier.

Making imitation paving stones

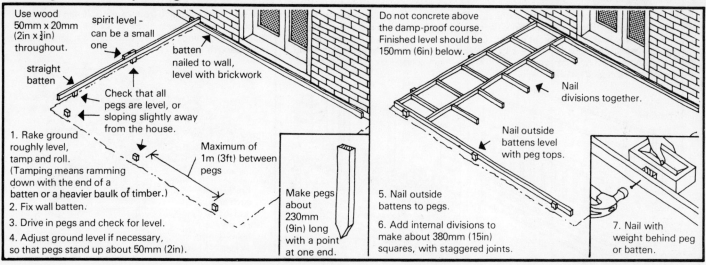

Use wood 50mm x 20mm (2in x ¾in) throughout.

spirit level - can be a small one

straight batten

batten nailed to wall, level with brickwork

Check that all pegs are level, or sloping slightly away from the house.

Maximum of 1m (3ft) between pegs

Make pegs about 230mm (9in) long with a point at one end.

1. Rake ground roughly level, tamp and roll. (Tamping means ramming down with the end of a batten or a heavier baulk of timber.)

2. Fix wall batten.

3. Drive in pegs and check for level.

4. Adjust ground level if necessary, so that pegs stand up about 50mm (2in).

Do not concrete above the damp-proof course. Finished level should be 150mm (6in) below.

Nail divisions together.

Nail outside battens level with peg tops.

5. Nail outside battens to pegs.

6. Add internal divisions to make about 380mm (15in) squares, with staggered joints.

7. Nail with weight behind peg or batten.

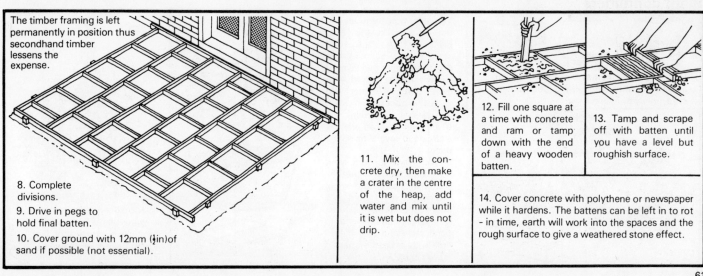

The timber framing is left permanently in position thus secondhand timber lessens the expense.

8. Complete divisions.

9. Drive in pegs to hold final batten.

10. Cover ground with 12mm (½in) of sand if possible (not essential).

11. Mix the concrete dry, then make a crater in the centre of the heap, add water and mix until it is wet but does not drip.

12. Fill one square at a time with concrete and ram or tamp down with the end of a heavy wooden batten.

13. Tamp and scrape off with batten until you have a level but roughish surface.

14. Cover concrete with polythene or newspaper while it hardens. The battens can be left in to rot - in time, earth will work into the spaces and the rough surface to give a weathered stone effect.

GARDEN JOBS
Window-boxes and plant holders

First measure the windowsill to decide on the size of the box you need. Cut the base, back, and end pieces from 150mm x 25mm (6in x 1in) board. If the box is to be more than 380mm (15in) long, you will also need to cut a piece to act as a centre support. Glue and pin the base to the ends, then glue and pin the back (and centre support if needed). Prime and paint the timber. Inside the box you can stand one or more polystyrene planting troughs, available from most gardening shops.

The wall holder is made from 25mm x 25mm (1in x 1in) softwood, screwed and glued as for the window-box. Make the openings just large enough to prevent the pots falling through.

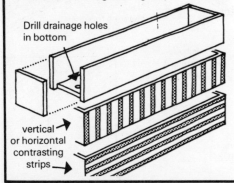

Drill drainage holes in bottom

vertical or horizontal contrasting strips

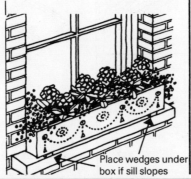

Place wedges under box if sill slopes

brackets at each end and in the centre (same length as side of holder)

Plant containers

Less expensive containers are becoming available in attractive designs, but you still save money by improvising.

You can transform an old bath or sink like this. First paint with PVA adhesive and sprinkle with sand. When dry, trowel on a thin layer of cement mortar mixed with equal parts of water and PVA adhesive. An inexpensive plastic tub treated this way can pass for a stone tub several times the price!

If you want to turn your containers round so that the plants in flower are more prominent, stand them on a board supported by castors.

If it is difficult for you to bend, raise your containers a little with a base of paving stones or bricks.

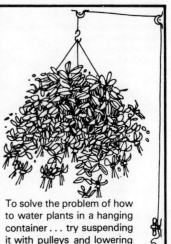

To solve the problem of how to water plants in a hanging container... try suspending it with pulleys and lowering it.

Transforming a small backyard

pots in plastic wall-rings
sunblinds
tub plants on trellis
more attractive door glazing
hanging basket
window boxes

I have seen unbelievably ugly backyards transformed into very attractive gardens with quite simple ideas. Even if there is no room for a lawn, a paved area with tubs, shrubs, and flower containers can give the effect of a well-ordered garden which is easy to keep.

Here is the view looking towards the house.

I suggest you paint a neat, white rectangle on the wall behind the dustbins and on the concrete beneath them. Then paint the dustbins themselves in bright colours - emulsion will do. This will remind others not to leave rubbish lying about. You could even grow a climbing plant (wisteria, clematis) behind the bins.

built-up bed
break corner of slab for smaller plants
slab left out to provide plant bed
shrub set in cobble stones

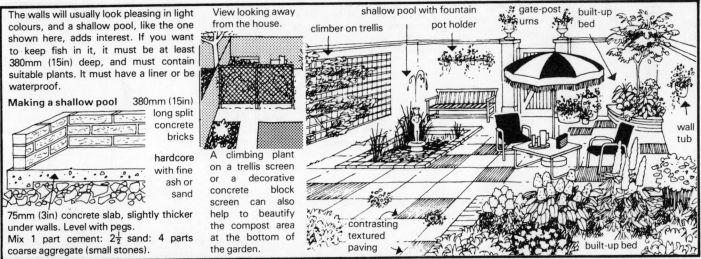

The walls will usually look pleasing in light colours, and a shallow pool, like the one shown here, adds interest. If you want to keep fish in it, it must be at least 380mm (15in) deep, and must contain suitable plants. It must have a liner or be waterproof.

Making a shallow pool

380mm (15in) long split concrete bricks

hardcore with fine ash or sand

75mm (3in) concrete slab, slightly thicker under walls. Level with pegs.
Mix 1 part cement: $2\frac{1}{2}$ sand: 4 parts coarse aggregate (small stones).

View looking away from the house.

A climbing plant on a trellis screen or a decorative concrete block screen can also help to beautify the compost area at the bottom of the garden.

climber on trellis
shallow pool with fountain
pot holder
gate-post urns
built-up bed

wall tub

contrasting textured paving

built-up bed

GARDEN JOBS
Keeping plants watered

You will need a plastic container to make this self-watering device. Clean it thoroughly; make a hole in the top and thread through a thin bootlace which has been soaked in water. This lace acts as a syphon. (An absorbent wadding is available which is more effective.) Tie a small rust-proof weight on to the lace to keep one end on the floor of the container. Bury the other end in the earth, taking it as low as possible. If there is room, bury the whole device in the earth. Use a filler with a small spout or funnel to fill the container with water.

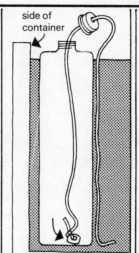

side of container

Use this method for watering several plants simultaneously, by running laces from one raised free-standing container. This will water the plants for a fairly long period.

Fitting a water butt

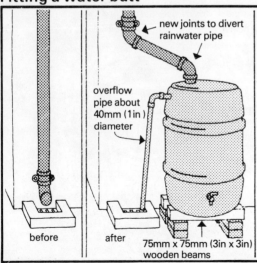

new joints to divert rainwater pipe

overflow pipe about 40mm (1in) diameter

before

after

75mm x 75mm (3in x 3in) wooden beams

Support water butt on columns of bricks and wooden beams, high enough to allow a watering can under the tap. If ground slopes, adjust the thickness of the beams or put packing under them. One or two plastic joints can divert the gutter pipe and take it through a hole in the lid, made with a hole saw or a tank cutter. But since these are tools you are unlikely to use very often, use a simple auger file instead. Screw it through to make the first hole and then file inside a guide line marked round the pipe you are going to fit.

Screw auger in to penetrate

Then file round the guide line

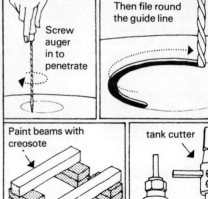

Paint beams with creosote

bricks

tank cutter

hole saw

Car emergencies

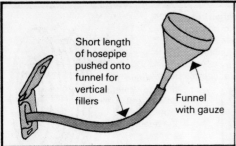

Short length of hosepipe pushed onto funnel for vertical fillers

Funnel with gauze

Running out of petrol Main danger is that sediment may be sucked through engine. Allow time for electric pump to operate.

It is possible to prime carburettor by lifting air filter and very carefully pouring in a tablespoonful of petrol. A funnel with a gauze is desirable when filling from a can. Be careful of the danger of fire.

Boiling radiator Allow time for cooling before removing cap. It is dangerous to lift the cap too soon.

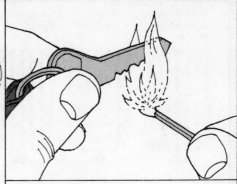

Frozen door locks heating the key with a match or just blowing on the lock with warm breath sometimes works.

If the car catches fire
1 Stop and switch off immediately.
2 Abandon car.
3 If flames have not yet started disconnect battery.
4 If flames are seen lift bonnet a fraction and fan fire extinguisher from side to side. Throwing open the bonnet and trying to beat out the flames is unlikely to succeed and is dangerous.

If the windscreen shatters
1 Avoid jerking the steering wheel or panic-braking.
2 If there is no clear-view zone, with clenched fist and straight arm smartly punch a hole through the glass in front of you to restore vision.
3 Pull into the side and stop.
4 The law requires full forward vision, so all the glass fragments must be removed before driving on. Do not leave glass on the road or verge.
5 When driving without a windscreen wind up all windows and increase speed only until the air pressure inside the car is neutral. This point is often marked by a faint fluttering in the air inside the car. If you try to drive faster the rear window may pop out.
6 Carrying a plastic emergency windscreen is a good idea.

If you burst a tyre
1 Keep a firm hold of the steering wheel and steer a straight course.
2 If the puncture is in a rear tyre pump the brakes firmly and draw into the side.
3 If the trouble is in a front tyre, brake as gently as possible (braking throws the weight of the car on to the affected wheel).

4 Switch on hazard lights as early as possible.

If you get stuck
In mud:
1 Use high gears and low revs, don't skid the wheels.
2 Try rocking the car between reverse and second gear to lift the wheel out of the hole.
3 Lay a track of scrub (bracken, heather, dry grass, hay) in front of each wheel, or lay down sacks, wire netting.

In sand:
1 Keep revs as low as possible, using high gears and taking care not to skid the wheels.
2 Lay down a track of sacks or wire netting.
3 Once you get moving try not to stop.

Correct pressures are essential. A hand gauge is sometimes more accurate than a gauge in a garage.

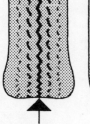  

Tyres are too soft. They create heat and can wear walls.

Too hard. The tread may be worn unevenly and the grip loose.

Correct. The tread grips the road firmly.

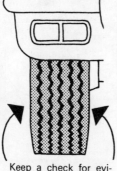

Keep a check for evidence of damaged walls. The damage inside is often worse than the damage you can see.

It is very easy to forget to check your tyres and to go on running till the treads have worn below the regulation 1mm depth (you can buy a tyre gauge which is also a depth gauge).

Check uneven wear at the front. If slightly out of correct track, tyre is being dragged sideways and will wear badly.

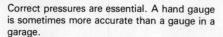

It is sound practice to carefully ease out all stones lodged in the tread.

Never put radial-ply tyres on the front with cross-ply tyres on the rear, or mix the types on the same axle.

Changing a wheel

Choose solid, level ground if you can, but don't drive on a flat tyre. Make sure the hand brake is on and that the jack is properly located at jacking point, and is on the level.

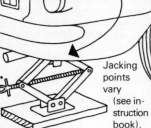

Jacking points vary (see instruction book).

Use wood under jack on soft ground.

Chock a wheel on a steep slope.

Don't leave door open. Prise off the hub-cap with a screwdriver or the end of the wheelbrace and loosen all nuts before you jack the wheel right off the ground. A combined torch and warning light is important for safety if you are in an exposed position.

If a garage has over-tightened the nuts, you can get extra leverage on the wheelbrace with two pieces of wood, bars, or spanners.

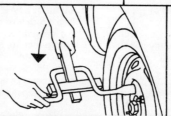

Screw all nuts on finger tight, tighten lightly with the wheelbrace, and tighten finally with the wheel on the ground.

It will help to keep the jack greased.

Remember the spare tyre when checking tyre pressures.

SPRAY GREASE

Rust protection

There are now several systems for carrying out thorough rust-prevention treatment, many of which give a guarantee. The material most in use contains a water repellent to drive out damp, a protective deposit (which often insulates and is therefore good for ignition systems), and a lubricant. You can buy rust-protecting products with a heavier wax deposit, which can be sprayed inside any specially vulnerable parts, such as car doors (door trims usually unclip: don't forget the window mechanism), around wheel arches and behind chrome strips. You will need to wire-brush first. Undersealing is a possible D.I.Y. job but is messy. Vigorous brushing is needed before applying one of the compounds made specially for sealing, some of which can be applied to damp surfaces. These sealing compounds will withstand some scouring by spray from the road, even in snowy conditions when spray often contains an element of salt. I am afraid I have nothing to suggest for exhaust systems, apart from investing in expensive stainless steel.

← syringe type sprayer

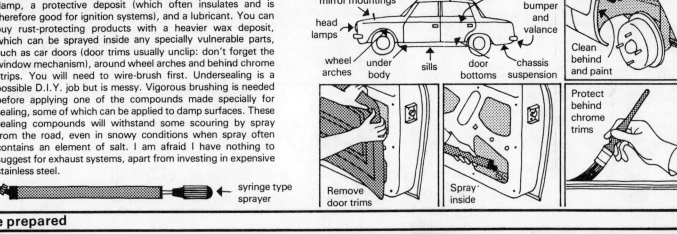

WHERE RUST ATTACKS

mirror mountings
gutters
behind trims
head lamps
bumper and valance
wheel arches
under body
sills
door bottoms
chassis suspension

Spray wheel arches
Clean behind and paint
Protect behind chrome trims
Remove door trims
Spray inside

Be prepared

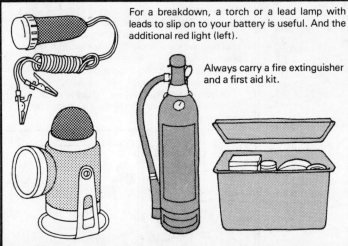

For a breakdown, a torch or a lead lamp with leads to slip on to your battery is useful. And the additional red light (left).

Always carry a fire extinguisher and a first aid kit.

Tyre spray increases traction on snow and ice. It lasts 3-4km (2-3 miles).

An accident-warning triangle is handy. Also a first-aid kit and an approved and serviced fire extinguisher.

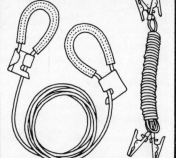

A nylon tow rope, or plastic-covered steel wire, a pair of jump leads for getting a start from someone else's battery can often help you out of trouble. As can improvised equipment in snowy weather, e.g. a couple of old sacks.

This is how to set about a simple rust repair job on an area of metal which is not structural. Use masking tape to protect surrounding coachwork. Scrape and sand rusted area as clean as possible. An electric sander or wire brush is useful.

Break or cut off badly rusted pieces. Tap edges of hole inwards.

double masking tape on door

← sander

If there is much open space, insert a piece of small-mesh expanded metal or perforated zinc covered with mixed synthetic resin filler (wear protective gloves), holding with a screw, to pull back against the inner surface. When filler sets, remove the screw and apply more filler with flexible piece of plastic, building it up in stages if much is needed. File and sand off surplus filler, finishing with a fine grade wet-and-dry sandpaper, smoothing the perimeter to an irregular edge.

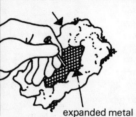

expanded metal

Allow to set

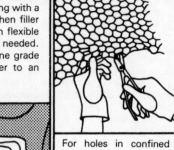

For holes in confined spaces you can use screwed-up chicken wire.

Sand down using rubber block

flexible plastic for spreading filler

You will need two or three coats of cellulose with a light rub down with fine wet-or-dry sandpaper. Wash with water between each coat. Smooth the final coat with a rubbing-down compound. Do not polish for three or four weeks. Using a non-cellulose paint over an original cellulose finish can cause severe bubbling which would have to be abraded completely before respraying. Faded paintwork is difficult as standard aerosol colours can't be mixed.

Rasp and sand the repair so that it follows the car's contours. Build it up with synthetic resin filler, and try again if you get it too hollow. Use a traffic film remover on the surrounding bodywork and protect with newspaper held on with masking tape.

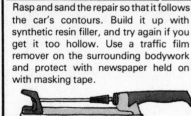

paper

paper →

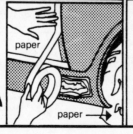

Brush or spray on primer. When spraying, hold the aerosol about 230mm (9in) away. Release the button at the end of each stroke and spray thinly. Rub this down with medium-fine wet-or-dry sand-paper.

Overlap original paint here.

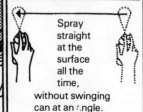

Spray straight at the surface all the time, without swinging can at an angle.

Repairing small dents

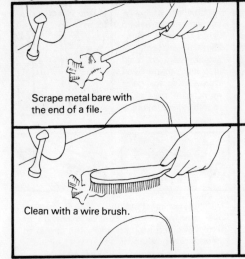

Scrape metal bare with the end of a file.

Mix up filler powder and resin (sold at motorists' shops).

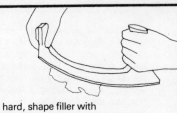

When hard, shape filler with a Surform shaper (curved if possible).

Clean with a wire brush.

Smooth it in with a flexible filler knife, leaving it slightly above the surrounding surface.

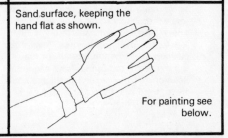

Sand surface, keeping the hand flat as shown.

For painting see below.

Touching up scratches

These are easy to deal with, but without care the car can look worse than it did before. First sand down the area of the scratch so that no ridges can be felt. Follow the instructions for shaking up aerosol in containers before you use them. First spray on a grey primer coat.

Spray on at least three coats of the appropriate colour. (You can buy sprays for most standard colours). Rub down all but the last coat, which should be polished.

Lesser scratches can sometimes be touched up quite neatly with a touching up kit which contains a small brush. Occasionally a scrape looks bad, but it is only the paint of the gatepost or whatever that has come off on your car. This can be removed with a metal polish or rubbing down compound.

Move the spray can of primer evenly across the repair 230-300mm (9-12in) from the surface.

Rub down primer coat with fine or medium wet-and-dry paper, keeping it wet.

YOUR CAR
Driving in comfort

Car manufacturers must compromise with the design of seats since it is impossible to produce a seat that is ideal for every occupant. This is an important aspect of driving since uncomfortable seating can lead to fatigue and stress and reduced driving efficiency. More seats are now made with adjustable back rests, which helps a great deal but does not solve the problem. If your seat is too low you will probably suffer from pains in your knees, shoulders or back through straining to see over the bonnet. A strap-on cushion might be the answer, or rebuilding the seat if the springs have sagged. A solution to your seating problems could be to buy a seat from a breaker's yard — it might fit you better.

inadequate thigh support

pushed forward by top roll

inadequate lumbar support

inadequate back support

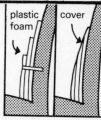

plastic foam   cover

Right: for a badly-shaped seat try making up a cushion. Tape 25mm (1 in) layers of plastic foam to build up the shape you want. When you get it right, glue the layers together and make a cover.

Difficulty in reaching the controls may be overcome by fitting a gear-lever extension, or firmly wedging a board under the carpet to lift your heels, or repositioning seat runners.

Garage tips

Not many of us have garages with room to spare. Usually the garage is fitted up with so much equipment that the car gets in only with difficulty. Driving close to obscured objects on the nearside is easier with a mirror on the wall adjusted to show where you are.

To avoid damaging doors against the side of the garage, nail or hang lengths of old hosepipe along the wall or stick on two or three polystyrene ceiling tiles, or strips of carpet. You can hang a piece of carpet between two cars.

To tell you just how far you can go before touching things stored at the end of the garage, hang a tennis ball, or a piece of metal, from the roof so when it touches the windscreen you know you are in.

Painting the floor with a coloured sealer smartens your garage and seals in cement dust, but get rid of oil drips first (use a proprietary oil remover). A discarded tea-tray is useful for catching drips; removable absorbent paper taped on to a panel of hardboard looks neat.

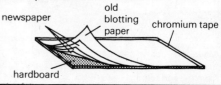

newspaper   old blotting paper   chromium tape

hardboard

Dealing with skids

Skidding to the right

Steer right

Steer left

Skidding to the left

Skidding is caused by excessive speed, or braking, cornering, gear changing, deceleration which is too violent for the surface you are on. Practice on a skid pan is helpful: ask your local authority if they have one. Or, if you are a member, ask the AA or RAC. Watch for hazards such as ice (steering will become very light), frost, mud, fallen leaves, loose shingle or grit, and light rain after a dry spell. Lower your speed to give a margin of safety and try to position the car when entering bends to allow room for a possible skid. Having done this, your driving will be more relaxed. Early recognition of skidding is essential to help you deal with skids.

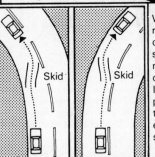

Skid

Skid

With front-engined, rear-wheel drive cars, a rear-wheel skid is most common. Steer in the direction of the skid. If over-correction produces a skid in the opposite direction, correct in the same way.

This often happens . . . driver A saw the danger, braked in panic and skidded into a head-on collision, when he could have squeezed through without braking hard.

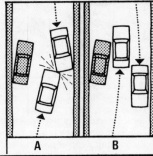

A   B

I have already suggested that when conditions are slippery, you should brake, accelerate, corner and change gear particularly gently. If enforced sudden hard braking should cause the wheels to lock, the tyres will cease to grip and the brakes become totally useless. Release the brakes and apply more gently. Dabbing the brake pedal gently on and off is the most effective way of getting a grip on a slippery road.

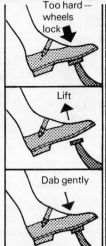

Too hard — wheels lock

Lift

Dab gently

Four-wheel skid

Front-wheel skid

In a four-wheel skid caused by harsh braking, or a front-wheel skid caused by harsh acceleration or locking steering over too hard, the car will proceed forward, or follow the camber, out of control. No steering movement can correct this. Do not alter the steering direction, instead decelerate gently, till the wheels grip. (Rapid deceleration might cause the car to spin - clockwise on a right-hand bend and vice versa). A rear-wheel skid, as described above, can be corrected by steering in the direction of the skid.

Spin

Skid

Tyre blow-outs can be dangerous, particularly on front wheels. A firm grip on the steering wheel helps you resist the resultant swerve, which may be violent. Do not brake fiercely or decelerate abruptly, this could cause a spin. As already suggested, practice in dealing with skids is vital.

YOUR CAR
When the car won't start

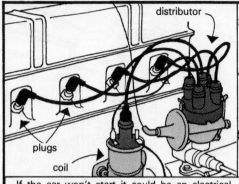

distributor

plugs

coil

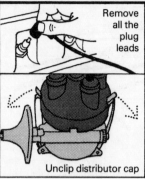

Remove all the plug leads

Unclip distributor cap

Remove lead from coil

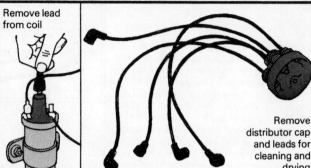

Remove distributor cap and leads for cleaning and drying

If the car won't start it could be an electrical failure. Turn off ignition, then check leads from coil to distributor, distributor to sparking plugs, for looseness. Tighten the lead coming from the coil by pulling back rubber sleeve, and screwing down central cap or pushing lead in.

If car still won't start, wipe all leads and spark plug caps with a dry rag. Release the two clips holding distributor cap in position and wipe inside of cap with dry rag. Replace cap and start car.

(A special damp repelent may be used—see below.)

Warning take care not to muddle plug leads.

Damp

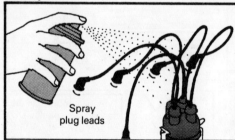

Spray plug leads

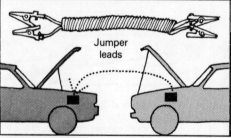

Jumper leads

Tap or tighten

In certain conditions damp can penetrate the plug wires particularly if these are faulty. Remedy—wipe wires and spray with water inhibiting fluid from an aerosol can.
Leave short interval between starting attempts. If the battery is flat, jumper cables will enable you to borrow current from someone else's battery. As soon as your engine has started the dynamo should be putting current in.

When the battery is well charged but the starter does not turn, this is often due to a bad connection on the battery earth lead. Tightening the nut or just a slight tap may cure this and you can have the connection removed and cleaned some time later. See right.

Further checks on wiring—make sure no wire have become disconnected from the coil or distributor.

Over-choking
Too much pumping on the accelerator (which squirts petrol into the carburettor) or excessive use of the choke can make it impossible to start the car. Leave for a few minutes then spin the engine with the starter with the accelerator pressed right down and no choke. Occasionally it is necessary to leave the car for a period until the condition puts itself right.

Anti-freeze

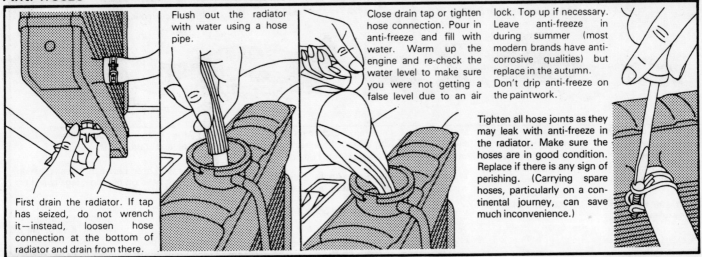

First drain the radiator. If tap has seized, do not wrench it—instead, loosen hose connection at the bottom of radiator and drain from there.

Flush out the radiator with water using a hose pipe.

Close drain tap or tighten hose connection. Pour in anti-freeze and fill with water. Warm up the engine and re-check the water level to make sure you were not getting a false level due to an air lock. Top up if necessary. Leave anti-freeze in during summer (most modern brands have anti-corrosive qualities) but replace in the autumn. Don't drip anti-freeze on the paintwork.

Tighten all hose joints as they may leak with anti-freeze in the radiator. Make sure the hoses are in good condition. Replace if there is any sign of perishing. (Carrying spare hoses, particularly on a continental journey, can save much inconvenience.)

Winter car care

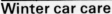

Here are some useful hints that could get you mobile without trouble on icy mornings.

If you cannot get the key into the door or boot locks during a cold spell, hold a lighted match under the lock.

To keep the locks free from frost, use penetrating oil.

Keep de-icing fluid handy for screens and windows if you don't keep them covered overnight.

Keep anti-freeze screen washing solvent in screen-washer bottle. Make sure it suits your screen washer.

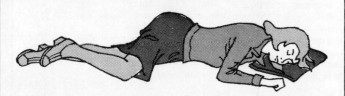

Unconcious accident victim placed on side.

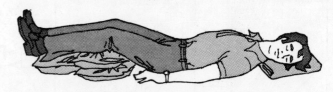

Person in a faint with legs on cushions, head on side

Except for minor accidents medical aid should be called as quickly as possible. Hospitals', ambulance, and doctors' numbers should be by the telephone, but you can always use 999 in an emergency. Keep a first aid box readily available.

Burns and scalds Cold running water applied quickly relieves pain.

Major burns Do not remove clothing or apply anything. Cover with clean light sheet dressing. Lay down and keep warm. Get to hospital.

Wounds and bleeding Apply pressure to wound to stop bleeding (can be fatal if severe).

Unconsciousness Turn on to one side to avoid choking. Give nothing by mouth.

Fractures Put patient at rest. Immobilise limb.

Shock After injury or sudden illness, keep patient warm and comfortable.

Fainting Sit with head between knees. When in faint lay down, head on one side, legs raised on cushions.

Electric shock Do not touch till current is switched off or plug pulled out. Kiss of life if breathing has stopped.

Gas asphyxiation Turn off supply. Avoid naked lights. Hold your breath and get patient to fresh air.

Nose bleeding Sit down. Pinch nose and apply cold compress.

Poisoning If pain in mouth and throat (possibly stomach) and damage to lips and tongue. Do *not* make vomit. Give lots of milk.

Sprains Cold compress, firm bandage. If doubtful treat for fracture.

Stings Remove if possible. Mild antiseptic. Mouth stings can be serious.

Shock After any injury or illness other than minor ones, lay on bed, keep quiet and warm (not with hot water bottles). Give nothing to drink.

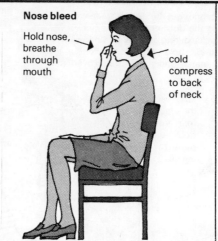

Nose bleed

Hold nose, breathe through mouth →

← cold compress to back of neck

A short course with your local St. John's Ambulance Brigade is invaluable.

Rescue from drowning

In the United Kingdom there are about 1,000 deaths from drowning every year, and included in that figure are many who have gone to the rescue of others. Do not fling yourself into the water without fully considering the situation. Try to reach the person in the water with anything you can hold on to, even a sweater.

If you can't reach the victim from the bank, throw in something which floats.

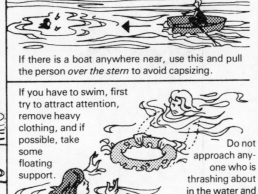

If there is a boat anywhere near, use this and pull the person *over the stern* to avoid capsizing.

If you have to swim, first try to attract attention, remove heavy clothing, and if possible, take some floating support. Do not approach anyone who is thrashing about in the water and shouting. Push the support towards them and stand by.

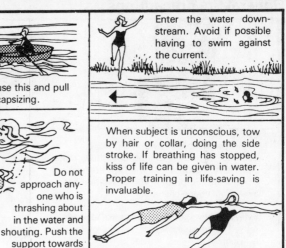

Enter the water downstream. Avoid if possible having to swim against the current.

When subject is unconscious, tow by hair or collar, doing the side stroke. If breathing has stopped, kiss of life can be given in water. Proper training in life-saving is invaluable.

The kiss of life

Open mouth and pinch nostrils

Breathing may cease for a number of reasons - electric shock, asphyxiation by gas, near-drowning or even being hit by a cricket ball.

Don't crowd around the victim. Call doctor and ambulance immediately. Remove false teeth, see that tongue is in front of mouth. Tilt head back, lift chin, open mouth and (except with young children) pinch nostrils. Cover mouth with your own (for young children, nostrils as well) and blow gently till chest rises. Then remove your mouth till chest falls, and repeat every five seconds. If chest fails to rise, try again with head further back. Get relays to carry on for an hour if necessary. Be gentle with a child as you can over-expand the lungs.

For adults - cover only the mouth

For young children - cover mouth and nostrils with your mouth, and remember, be gentle.

SAFETY FIRST
General fire precautions

Avoid leaving children alone.
See that proper fireguards are fitted, that paraffin fires cannot be tipped up, that night-dresses are fire proof and matches are kept away from young children.

Extinguishers should be serviced regularly, refilled when necessary, and kept prominently displayed.

Check on whether an electric blanket is made to be used under or over the sheets and is used correctly. Improper use is very dangerous. Switch off and unplug if folding up.

Safety for children

In 1972 there were 596 fatal accidents in the home involving children under fourteen.

☐ Are your fires properly guarded?

☐ Do you turn saucepan handles inwards?

☐ Is your kettle flex as short as possible?

☐ Are dangerous drugs kept in a cabinet safe from small hands (see p.79)?

☐ Is their nightwear flameproof?

☐ Are dangerous stairs fitted with child safety gates?

☐ Are all bottles of detergents, bleach, poisons, medicine clearly marked and locked away?

☐ Are all weedkillers and other garden chemicals locked away and not left around in milk bottles or soft-drink bottles?

☐ Always unplug electrical appliances when left unattended.

☐ Keep heaters out of children's reach.

☐ Are all your electric outlet sockets properly shielded?

Dealing with fires

Many serious fires are started by smaller fires which could easily have been extinguished. However, you should never tackle a fire yourself unless you think you can extinguish it immediately. You can use water on most fires, even on a paraffin heater, but **NEVER** on live electrical equipment or on burning fat (see below).

Avoid knocking heater over.

When clothing is on fire, lie down immediately and, if possible, roll yourself in a blanket, rug, towel or other clothing. Get medical aid for burns and shock.

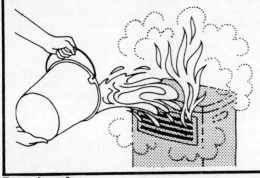

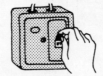

Small fires can be dealt with by fire blankets .
If electrical equipment catches fire, unplug or switch off at the mains before using water. A television set can be covered with a' wet blanket when unplugged.

If any fire is too big, close the door to confine the flames and smoke, get everyone out of the house and call the fire brigade. If trapped, keep door closed, place rolled-up blanket against bottom of door, crawl under the smoke, open a window, and shout for help.

Burning fat

Don't run with it outside or put it under the tap. Smother the flames. Use whichever of these three methods is most quickly available. Slide a wet towel or fire blanket over the pan . . .

Swamp the pan with flour . . .

Cover the pan with a saucepan lid.

SAFETY FIRST
Safety with electricity

If you follow the rules and requirements of the electricity board, you can be reasonably certain that you will be in no danger from any electrical equipment. Here are some of the points that they make.

Careless use of electric blankets is an increasing cause of serious accidents. Blankets need regular servicing (best in the spring when manufacturers are less busy). An underblanket should be used only to pre-heat your bed. Thermostatically controlled overblankets are available which can be left on all night. Never leave any sort of electric blanket folded and switched on.

Portable mains appliances must never be used in bathrooms, and no power sockets are allowed in a bathroom or within reach of water. The only safe fire is a protected one, *well out of reach,* with a pull-cord switch.

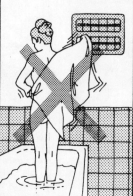

Your electrical installation must be properly earthed. The electricity board or a registered electrician will check your system if necessary. Other than double-insulated appliances, which are marked ☐ and shavers for use with special shaver sockets, all other appliances must be properly earthed. Accidents are caused by bad plug connections, plugs wired to the wrong colour code (see page 18), detached earth wires, and chafed wires. Check grommets where wires enter metal appliances and see there is no chafing.

Any dampness or the close proximity of water is an added danger when using an electric appliance. (Outlet sockets should not be fitted near a sink, for instance.) If you get a shock while in contact with a damp surface, your body can receive a much more dangerous charge of electricity. Do not touch a person who has been electrocuted if he or she is still touching the appliance with the current still on. Switch off or pull out the plug immediately. Call a doctor and ambulance. Give the kiss of life if breathing has stopped (see page 75).

Safety with gas

If there is a faint smell of gas, trace and deal with the cause - possibly a pilot light has gone out or a burner has been left on. It's good practice to make a quick check every time you leave the kitchen that all gas taps that should be off *are* off - particularly last thing at night.

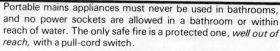

Open all windows and doors and wait for the smell to go. Anyone overcome by gas should be taken to open air quickly and have their clothes loosened. If breathing has ceased give kiss of life (see p. 75) while ambulance and doctor are being called.

Extinguish all naked flames and electric fires.

If the smell persists or is very strong, turn off the main gas tap. Keep fires and lighters extinguished, doors and windows open. Call the local gas board (day or night). Keep the emergency number by your telephone.

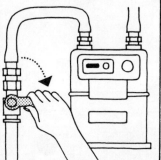

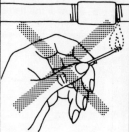

Never test with a naked flame. Use washing-up liquid on joints instead: bubbles will indicate a leak. This method can also be used when testing for bottled-gas leaks in a caravan.

Keeping out burglars

There is a very large number of anti-burglar devices on the market that can be fitted easily. You can obtain valuable free advice from the police or your local locksmith. I don't want to advocate any half-measures, but if you are going away and failed to buy anything, you can screw up wooden doors and windows with ordinary screws (any windows not required for ventilation can be left permanently fixed).

Start the hole with the drill at right angles, then drill at an angle.

Key-operated window lever lock for metal casement. **Needs fitting with self-tapping screws slightly larger than holes you drill.**

Key operated window - stay lock.

Lock the doors on all internal rooms and remove keys.

Key-operated mortice bolt for wooden sashes or doors.

Door catch – simple device for internal doors without locks. Folds over and clicks into position.

On front door . . . replace night latch with a deadlock, or add a mortice lock.

Don't leave a ladder about.

A final check before you go: no fanlights or windows left open, no keys on strings or hidden under the mat, and - *do the neighbours know you will be away?*

door

door jamb

Child-proof cabinet and gate

For bathroom cabinets, medicine cabinets and cleaning cupboards, I have patented a device which no child has been known to operate, but which is quick and easy for an adult to use. This is fitted to cabinets sold in the shops (by Meltex), but is something you can make yourself. It is based on the simple fact that an adult finger is longer than a child's finger. All you have to do is to fix the simple spring catch shown behind the door and then bore a 25mm (1in) hole through the door so that your finger will just reach the catch through the hole. Enclosing the catch in a small plywood box makes it doubly secure. A similar method can be used on an ordinary gate catch or a child gate to protect children from dangerous stairs.

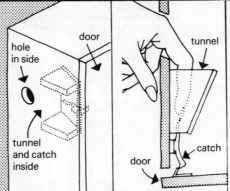

hole in side

door

tunnel and catch inside

tunnel

door

catch

Medicine cabinet: your finger reaches the catch through a hole in the side of the cabinet, as shown in the view from above in the right-hand drawing.

Gate: Plywood or exterior gate hardboard nailed or screwed and glued to two battens - just wide enough for your finger to reach through. Paint wood to protect it.

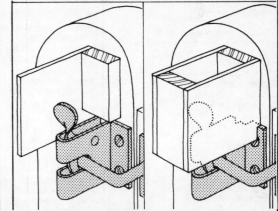

Index